Brian has had a big impact on our family. My kids have been in a kids ministry the last several years that uses The Gospel Project—a curriculum that is centered on the gospel that Brian helps form every week. Not only are they learning stories in the Bible, but also they are learning how these point us to Jesus. And my kids, like me, need Him to change and refresh their hearts. As a dad, I am very thankful for the ministry philosophy outlined in this book.

Eric Geiger, vice president, LifeWay Christian Resources

I'm thrilled whenever I see veteran kidmin leaders like Brian Dembowczyk sounding the alarm against a moralistic substitute for the gospel, and leading the charge to give our children the Story of the Bible, not just the stories of the Bible. Transformation of the heart, brought about only by an encounter with Jesus through the gospel, should be our goal when we serve our children. I'm thankful for the way Brian steers us in the right direction.

Trevin Wax, Bible and Reference Publisher for B&H, managing editor of The Gospel Project, author of *Gospel-Centered Teaching: Showing Christ in All the Scripture*

Every Christian leader and parent understands the tremendous privilege and responsibility of passing on the faith to the next generation. The statistics tell us that only 30 percent of kids will remain steadfast in the faith as adults. These numbers should both alarm us and bolster our commitment to disciple our children. In *Gospel-Centered Kids Ministry*, Brian Dembowczyk offers a clarion call to the church that is not full of gimmicks and fads. The answer isn't guilt-heavy moralism or behavior modification. The answer is found in applying the beauty and power of the gospel of Jesus Christ to little hearts. Dembowczyk makes this case with deep theology and a warm pastoral heart. This book is a gift to the entire church.

Matthew Z. Capps (D.Min., Gordon-Conwell Theological Seminary), senior pastor, Fairview Baptist Church, Apex, North Carolina

BRIAN DEMBOWCZYK

GOSPEL CENTERED KIDS MINISTRY

How the gospel will transform your kids,
your church, your community,
and the world

PUBLISHING GROUP

NASHVILLE, TENNESSEE

Copyright © 2018 by B&H Publishing Group
Printed in the United States of American
All rights reserved.

978-1-5359-3955-3

Published by B&H Publishing Group
Nashville, Tennessee

Dewey Decimal Classification: C248.4
Subject Heading: CHRISTIAN LIFE / GOSPEL / DISCIPLESHIP

All Scripture quotations are taken from the
Christian Standard Bible® Copyright 2017 by Holman
Bible Publishers. Used by permission.

2 3 4 5 6 7 8 • 25 24 23 22 21

CONTENTS

PART 3: GOSPEL-CENTERED TRANSFORMATION

PART 4: GOSPEL-CENTERED MISSION

PART 5: GOSPEL-CENTERED LEADERS

PART 6: GOSPEL-CENTERED PARENTS

INTRODUCTION

On April 11, 1970, at 2:13 p.m., 203,400 gallons of kerosene and 318,000 gallons of liquid oxygen were ignited. The resulting fury was harnessed to produce 7.5 million pounds of thrust to lift the Saturn V rocket off Launch Pad 39A at Cape Canaveral in central Florida and, after two more controlled explosions, propel it into space.

Along for the ride that day was the three astronaut crew of *Apollo 13*, Commander James Lovell Jr., Command Module Pilot John Swigert Jr., and Lunar Module Pilot Fred Haise Jr. *Apollo 13*'s mission, to land on the moon, followed in the quite literal footsteps of *Apollo 11* and *Apollo 12*. This was billed as just the third moon landing ever. The previous two landings had only taken place within the last nine months.

At 9:08 p.m. on April 13, just a few minutes after the crew had completed a TV broadcast, they heard a loud noise and felt a vibration. A warning light caught John Swigert's attention. He immediately radioed in the famous, although often modified line, "Houston, we've had a problem here."

What no one knew at the time was a small explosion had knocked out one of the main craft's two oxygen tanks and had damaged the other. The situation was dire. The oxygen the crew needed to breathe was rapidly venting into space, and electrical power and the water supply were also severely depleted.

At the time, the crew was 200,000 miles from Earth—roughly the distance around the world eight times.

Ninety minutes after the explosion, with oxygen plummeting toward zero, the crew quickly put a plan in place to use the Lunar Module (LM) as a lifeboat to keep them alive. The crew was instructed to shut down the Command Module (CM), move into the LM, and close the hatch between the two.

The LM had plenty of oxygen. The craft had independent tanks designed for the moon descent that would provide plenty of breathing hours for the crew. There were also ascent tanks available and two backpacks with extra oxygen for walking on the moon.

Oxygen wasn't a problem, but water and power certainly would be. Each of the three astronauts was limited to drinking only six ounces of water a day, less than a quarter of what each man would normally drink. As a result, the crew became dehydrated and lost just over 31 pounds of combined body weight, more than any other crew before them. Lovell dropped 14 pounds alone. Energy was also reduced to 20 percent of what would normally be used.

The crew soon discovered another problem, removing carbon dioxide from the LM. The lithium hydroxide canisters could sufficiently remove CO_2 for two men for two days. However, the LM now needed to remove the carbon dioxide produced by three men for about four days. There were enough filters on the CM, but yet another problem developed—the CM's system used square filters while the LM used round ones.

By the second day of the crew's escape to the LM, the carbon dioxide levels had risen to dangerous levels. There was only one thing NASA could do: figure out how to make a square peg fit into a round hole. The lives of the three astronauts were at stake. NASA teams on the ground got to work, thought outside of the box, and developed a procedure to use the square canisters with the round system using plastic bags, cardboard, and tape.

With the carbon dioxide emergency solved and the water and power rationed, there was still one lingering question to answer. And it was a big one.

How would the crew get back safely to Earth?

There were two parts to the answer. The first concerned navigation.

When the explosion occurred, the craft was on course for a lunar landing. Now, the goal was to return the craft to the trajectory needed to get it back to Earth. Yet again, there was a problem. The navigation system used the stars to determine direction, but the explosion had created a debris field around the ship, making it impossible to locate a reliable star. Once again, NASA was tasked to solve a problem and once again, they came through. An alternate process of using the sun for navigation was used to put the craft on the proper course back to Earth.

The second part of getting the crew safely back to Earth involved powering up the CM for re-entry. The LM could not be used to enter Earth's orbit. The CM was needed for that, but it had been shut down. NASA had to do something never done before: develop a routine to power up a craft in space using barely any electricity. What they came up with also had to be perfectly completed by a crew that was tired, cold, and dehydrated. Teams on the ground worked frantically on the problem and completed the process checklist.

It worked. Perfectly.

On April 17, 1970, the *Apollo 13* capsule splashed down into the warm waters of the Pacific Ocean near Samoa, and the astronauts were taken aboard the USS Iwo Jima.

James Lovell, John Swigert, and Fred Haise were back on Earth. What might have been NASA's greatest failure became one of its greatest victories.[1]

---

1. Sources: "Apollo 13," NASA Mission Pages [online] 8 July 2009 [cited 6 February 2017]. Available on the Internet: https://www.nasa.gov/missions Karl Tate. "NASA's Mighty Saturn V Moon Rocker Explained," 9 November 2012 [cited 6 February 2017]. Available on the Internet: http://www.space.com.

—PART 1—
WHEN THE GOSPEL IS IN THE MARGINS

CHAPTER 1

FAILURE IS NOT AN OPTION

"Failure is not an option."

That line was made famous by NASA Flight Director Gene Kranz during the *Apollo 13* mission. While we don't know if he really said it, the sentiment certainly was true of the NASA teams on the ground and the three astronauts in space in April 1970.

Loss of oxygen. Depleted power and water. Square carbon dioxide filters in round containers. Navigating without the stars. Powering up a cold and wet Command Module in space. Dehydration. Exhaustion.

Problem after problem was thrown at NASA over the course of the four days following an oxygen tank explosion. Any one of them was enough to make most people throw up their hands in despair and give up.

But not NASA.

For them, failure was not an option. The reason was simple. The stakes were too high. Three astronauts' lives hung in the balance. These three men, 200,000 miles from earth, were friends. They were also husbands, fathers, and sons. Failure meant their certain deaths. It was not an option.

Reducing water and power use by 20 percent? "We'll make it work. We have to. Failure is not an option!"

Make square filters work in round containers? "We'll make it work. We have to. Failure is not an option!"

Navigate using the sun? "We'll make it work. We have to. Failure is not an option!"

Power up a freezing craft in outer space for the first time ever? "We'll make it work. We have to. Failure is not an option!"

Gene Kranz may not have said it, but NASA certainly practiced it. This relentless pursuit of success is why the events surrounding the *Apollo 13* mission are often considered some of NASA's finest hours. Because failure was not an option, NASA turned a near tragedy into one of the most remarkable achievements of the program.

NASA resolved to do whatever was required to get their three astronauts home alive. Thanks to their determination, that's exactly what they accomplished.

CHAPTER 2

CHURCH, WE HAVE A PROBLEM

Failure wasn't an option for NASA, but if you look at the statistics, failure sure seems like it is an option for the church in America today.

According to LifeWay Research, roughly 70 percent of young adults drop out of church.[2] That means seven out of ten of the kids you love, serve, pray over, teach, mentor, cry with, laugh with, high five, and hug will walk away from the church when they are out of high school.

Interestingly, the research also indicates about two-thirds of those dropouts return to the church later on—perhaps when they have kids of their own. So, only about 23 percent of young

---

2. Ed Stetzer, "Dropouts and Disciples: How Many Students Are Really Leaving the Church?" *Christianity Today* (14 May 2014), accessed 6 February 2017. Available on the Internet: http://www.christianitytoday.com.

adults drop out for good. Let's be optimists and call that 20 percent.

According to those statistics, here's how your kids ministry breaks down right now:

- *Twenty percent of your kids* will walk away from the church for good.
- *Fifty percent of your kids* will leave the church for a season but return later on.
- *Thirty percent of your kids* will stay in the church.

Let those numbers sink in. In a few years, two out of every ten kids in your church will walk away for good.

Five more will leave the church for an extended period of time. They will remove themselves from a church family and dramatically reduce their ability to glorify God. Without the church's accountability and encouragement to guide them, these young adults will increasingly put themselves in the way of temptation.

Only three of the ten will stay connected to the church. Perhaps failure is not an option for the church today after all. It's not an option because it is reality.

So let's cut to the chase. Whose fault is it? Who is to blame for this failure?

Is it the parents' fault? God has given them the primary responsibility to disciple their kids, right? Did parents drop the ball?

Or is it the college and young adult ministry's fault? The dropout is occurring "on its watch," right? Is this ministry simply failing in its role to pick up the baton from the student ministry?

Speaking of student ministry, perhaps it's to blame. Student ministry has students for six to seven years—very formative years. Isn't this plenty of time to make sure kids are tethered to the church before they leave for college or to start a career?

What about pastors? Maybe they're to blame for not casting a vision of disciple-making to parents and ministry leaders and not equipping them to succeed.

While each of these may play a role in the dropout rate, there's one other ministry we have to put under the microscope, a ministry which may be key in reversing the trend of young adults leaving the church—kids ministry.

I know what you might be thinking. How in the world does kids ministry share in the responsibility for the dropout rate of young adults leaving the church years later? It's a great question. A fair question. In fact, I believe we will see a dramatic decrease in this dropout rate if we can successfully answer this question.

But first, we need to understand what this dropout rate really means.

CHAPTER 3

EMPTY PEWS AND EMPTY HEARTS

It would be a mistake to see this dropout rate simply as an indictment of the church. While it certainly may be in part, there's something much deeper at play. The church dropout is a symptom, albeit an important and harmful one, of a much more serious disease.

To see this, consider Hebrews 10:24–25, a passage often used to argue that believers need to be part of a local church.

> **And let us watch out for one another to provoke love and good works, not neglecting to gather together, as some are in the habit of doing, but encouraging each other, and all the more as you see the day approaching.**

There it is. We shouldn't neglect meeting together. The Bible instructs us to go to church. It doesn't get any clearer, right? At least this is how we often hear the argument phrased. Go to church because the Bible says to.

I fully embrace the complete authority of the Bible. If Scripture says to do something, I take it at face value. However, I also want to get to the why of the Bible's commands. If possible, I want to understand God's heart behind the command so that I can know Him more fully.

So let's break this passage down some and see if we can find God's heart behind this command.

Notice the three reasons the author of Hebrews gives for gathering together as a church. One comes right before the imperative, the other two right after it.

First, we gather "to provoke love and good works." The Greek word translated as *provoke* means to contend. Interestingly, it's found in just one other place in the New Testament—Acts 15:39—where it refers to the heated disagreement between Paul and Barnabas on whether to include Mark on a mission journey.

So when the writer of Hebrews is talking about provoking one another to love and good works, he means that we should be connecting deeply with one another so that we cannot sit still as believers. We have to do something. Our affections for Christ are stirred so deeply when we gather that we cannot help but love others as a result. We cannot help but seek to bring God glory through what we do and say.

This provoking happens as we proclaim the gospel to one another. Every time we gather, hearing and sharing the gospel should be central. And as we preach the gospel to one another, our affections will be stirred and expressed through love and good works.

"Encouraging each other" is the second reason believers should gather together. When we think of encouragement, we often think of positive, affirming statements. That is certainly part of encouragement, but it goes much deeper. You see, God isn't merely interested in the church being a rally for positive-thinking.

The Greek word translated as *encouraging* here is *parakaleo*—literally "to call alongside." That might not mean much until we connect this word with *paraclete*—"advocate" or "helper"—a common name the New Testament uses for the Holy Spirit. So the way we encourage one another in the church is to function in ways similar to the Holy Spirit.

We don't replace the Holy Spirit of course, but we do pattern our relationships in the church after His relationship with us. And what does the Holy Spirit do? He guides us and directs us. He convicts us of sin. He comforts and consoles us. He changes us. That involves more than merely saying affirming things, doesn't it?

God intends for us to gather together and put sin to death in our lives. We are to weep and mourn together. We are to laugh and celebrate together. We are

> We are to weep and mourn together. We are to laugh and celebrate together . . . We are to change. This is what it means to truly encourage one another.

to hold one another accountable toward our calling. We are to help one another live differently today than we did yesterday. We are to change. This is what it means truly to encourage one another. Left to ourselves, we are not strong enough to achieve any of these acts of transformation. This sanctification can only take place because Jesus calls us while we are sinners and provides us with His enabling righteousness. This is where the church differs from any other institution. While other human gatherings might seek to achieve behavior modification, only the church can experience gospel transformation.

The third reason for gathering together is more subtle, but no less important. Actually, the more we understand it, the greater we should desire to gather together. We gather together as we "see the day approaching."

The *day* is the return of Christ. As we consider that each day draws us closer to the return of Jesus, we are compelled to gather as the church. Why? Because we know time is short. Jesus is returning soon. This will be a great day for those of us who have trusted in Jesus, but it will be a terrible day for those who haven't.

That is why Christ's return prompts us to gather together more.

> We gather together to live on mission, something accomplished better together than alone.

We gather to carry out our mission to share the gospel with an unbelieving world so that many people can be spared from the wrath of God. We gather together to live on mission, something accomplished better together than alone.

So, why do we gather? We gather to proclaim the gospel, to live in meaningful community that spurs growth, and to be on mission together. Gospel, transformation, mission—three reasons, one imperative.

Dropping out of the church is far more than rejecting church culture. Walking away from the church is forsaking the gospel, refusing to be changed, and rejecting God's mission for us. Walking away from the church is actually walking away from Jesus and all He died for.

CHAPTER 4

KIDS MINISTRY: THE KEY TO KEEPING YOUNG ADULTS?

So let's get back to the question at hand—what does the dropout rate have to do with kids ministry? Here's what I believe is happening.

Young adults are leaving the church because we—parents, pastors, student leaders, kids leaders, teachers—have failed to give them the one thing that satisfies. We have failed to give them the gospel. The full, rich, beautiful gospel. We may have shared on multiple occasions a summary of the gospel and invited them to trust in Jesus, but we haven't done much else. We haven't connected the dots in our kids' and teens' hearts about how the entire Bible and all of life is about one thing—the gospel.

I believe 70 percent of our kids will walk away from the church as young adults because we've failed to anchor the gospel into their hearts as kids and teens. They walk away—some for good—because they haven't been given the one thing that will satisfy their souls. The one thing that will engage their imagination and stir their affections. We haven't given them Jesus.

I know that sounds harsh, but I share this with love and deep concern. I share it from serving in the trenches of kids ministry alongside you. We have to take a good long, hard look at our ministries and ask what we are teaching and modeling to our kids. What sort of foundation are we helping to lay in their minds and hearts?

Are we teaching the gospel to our kids? Are we teaching the fullness of the gospel by covering some of the more challenging Bible stories and talking about topics that we might normally want to skip over? Or are we teaching Bible stories out of context, gravitating toward only the safe and feel-good stories? Do our kids hear Jesus each week and understand how the Bible is really one big story about Him? Or do they only hear about Jesus when we talk about the New Testament?

Are we teaching kids what it means to find their identity in Christ and what He's done for them? Or are we teaching behavior modification by impressing upon kids the burden of living and performing in a certain way to please God? Are we creating space in our ministry where kids can recognize their sinfulness, be real about their sin, and embrace their desperate need of a Savior? Or is our main focus to create "good Christian kids"?

Are we helping kids see their purpose in life, a purpose that starts right now? Are we casting the lofty, God-given vision to our kids that they are ambassadors, placed by God in their neighborhoods, schools, sports teams, and even homes to be on mission for Him? Are we equipping them and supporting them for that mission?

Are we leading our kids in a way that models the gospel? Are we captivated by Christ, basking in God's grace? Are we appropriately transparent and on mission?

Are we equipping and encouraging parents as partners in ministry? Are we looking at our ministries holistically, seeking to balance times of teaching, training, and equipping with time for our leaders and families to pursue the gospel and be on mission?

As we explore the answers to these questions, we'll see that kids ministry is on the front lines of the fight against the dropout rates. In fact, gospel-centered kids ministry may be the key to stopping church dropout and transforming our kids, our families, our churches, our communities, and our world.

> Are we leading our kids in a way that models the gospel? Are we captivated by Christ, basking in God's grace? Are we appropriately transparent and on mission?

CHAPTER 5

ALL HANDS ON DECK

Let's be clear. We're in an "all hands on deck" crisis. The harm affecting those leaving churches, the Church itself, and the world presents too great a need for us to be passive. We cannot afford to wait for other parents or another ministry to fix what is wrong. We all need to be part of the solution. Whether you're a parent, kids ministry pastor or director, teacher, worship leader, or volunteer, you have a role to play in the solution. We all need to own it and work together toward it.

Can you imagine if the NASA team members on the ground would have dared to say it wasn't their fault that the astronauts were stranded in space? What if they then continued to go about their typical routine as if nothing was wrong. The thought is absurd, isn't it? The lives of three men hung in the balance. It was clearly an "all hands on deck" moment. Everyone rolled up their sleeves and did whatever it took to rescue those men.

How much more dire is our crisis? The eternal destination of thousands and thousands of boys and girls and men and women hangs in the balance. We need to do whatever it takes to do our part in rescuing them with the gospel.

This is exactly what Paul had in mind when he penned 1 Corinthians 9:19–23:

> **Although I am free from all and not anyone's slave, I have made myself a slave to everyone, in order to win more people. To the Jews I became like a Jew, to win Jews; to those under the law, like one under the law—though I myself am not under the law—to win those under the law. To those who are without the law, like one without the law—though I am not without God's law but under the law of Christ—to win those without the law. To the weak I became weak, in order to win the weak. I have become all things to all people, so that I may by every possible means save some. Now I do all this because of the gospel, so that I may share in the blessings.**

Do you see it? Paul was willing to do whatever it took. No sacrifice was too great. No work too difficult. No challenge too large. All with the singular focus of winning people to Christ. All for the gospel. Failure was not an option for Paul. And that is the attitude we must embrace in kids ministry.

CHAPTER 6

SO, IS THE CHURCH DOOMED?

The statistics don't look good for the church in America today. Most quantifiable indicators of church health are in decline. Attendance. Participation. Giving. You name it. So is the church really in that much trouble? Are we witnessing the death spiral of the American church? No, we are not. Not at all.

I am greatly excited and optimistic about the church's future. I don't want you to misunderstand my deep concern with the dropout rate as doom and gloom for the church. Yes, we have a serious problem to address, but that doesn't mean we need to be pessimistic. I'm more hopeful for the church than I ever have been before. And I'm not alone.

Many of us look at the landscape of the church and see something beautiful and encouraging taking place. We see a movement toward gospel-centeredness. Churches and individuals are intentionally focusing on the gospel story of God providing Jesus as the one and only solution for sin. The gospel is no longer being seen as merely a five-minute explanation of how to become a Christian; it is being taught as the sustaining foundation for what a relationship with Jesus looks like.

We see churches fighting to be authentic in conveying their desperate need for a Savior. A vital part of the gospel is recognizing our deep sinfulness and overwhelming need for God's grace. The masks of perfection that many have worn in the church are being thrown aside in favor of living authentically with one another as redeemed sinners. Sin is not celebrated, but it isn't swept under the rug either. People are not afraid to be who they really are—recovering sinners being transformed by God's grace.

> **The gospel is no longer being seen as merely a five-minute explanation of how to become a Christian; it is being taught as the sustaining foundation for what a relationship with Jesus looks like.**

Churches are also embracing their missional calling. The gospel always calls us to action; we cannot sit still. We've experienced the lavish grace and love of God, and we want others to experience it also. Everyday life takes on new meaning. The grocery store is not simply the place where food is purchased; it is a mission field. Our neighborhood is not just a comfortable place to live; it is a mission field.

Our kids ministries need to overflow with gospel-centeredness. For some, this will mean changing what we teach or the way we teach. For others, this will mean changing or even ending programs that are not driving kids toward the gospel. For still others, this will mean fostering authentic community with kids, families, and volunteers. And for others, this will mean getting outside of the walls of the church to be on mission.

It won't be easy. In fact, most likely it will be hard, demanding, controversial, tiring work. You may be tempted to question if it is worth it. And the answer will always be yes. Yes, it is worth it. The gospel is always worth it.

For the remainder of this book, we are going to delve into the following five key areas of kids ministry to see how we can be more gospel-centered in each:

- **Gospel-Centered Teaching.** What is the gospel, and how does it impact the way kids live for Christ as His followers?
- **Gospel-Centered Transformation.** How does the gospel change us, and what is our reason for living differently because of Jesus?
- **Gospel-Centered Mission.** How can we cast vision and train kids as missionaries right now?
- **Gospel-Centered Leaders.** What does a gospel-centered kids leader look like?
- **Gospel-Centered Parents.** What is the relationship between the church and the home? How can churches best partner with

parents in a relationship of mutual support and encouragement?

There is so much to be excited about. But above all, I'm optimistic and excited because of what Jesus said:

"I will build my church, and the gates of Hades will not overpower it." (Matt. 16:18)

Gates are defensive. If gates fail, it's because an aggressor attacked and overcame them. However, Jesus intends for us to be on the offensive. He intends for us to take the fight to the enemy. He never intended for us merely to duck and cover. As we charge toward the battle and fight for our kids, we do so with optimism and hope.

> **Jesus never intended for us merely to duck and cover.**

Gene Kranz of NASA may have had high expectations for the success of his program, but Jesus said it best when He told His Church, "Failure is not an option!"

—PART 2—
GOSPEL-CENTERED TEACHING

CHAPTER 7

FROM STORIES TO STORY: FINDING MEANING IN THE GOSPEL

They had so much to talk about. It was Easter Sunday—*the* Easter Sunday—and two followers of Jesus were making the seven-mile journey from Jerusalem to the town of Emmaus. One of the travelers was a man named Cleopas. The other is unnamed. The two talked excitedly with each other as they traveled along the dusty road toward Emmaus, trying to make sense of all they had experienced and heard over the past week.

Then Jesus showed up, but the men were prevented from recognizing Him. Jesus asked the pair what they were talking about.

The two came to a full stop and stood still, looking sad. "Uh, do you live under a rock?" replied Cleopas. (At least that's my version.) Cleopas actually said, "Are you the only visitor to Jerusalem who does not know the things that have happened there in these days?"

Jesus pressed in more. "What things?" He asked.

The two began to explain what had happened recently.

> So they said to him, "The things concerning Jesus of Nazareth, who was a prophet powerful in action and speech before God and all the people, and how our chief priests and leaders handed him over to be sentenced to death, and they crucified him. But we were hoping that he was the one who was about to redeem Israel. Besides all this, it's the third day since these things happened. Moreover, some women from our group astounded us. They arrived early at the tomb, and when they didn't find his body, they came and reported that they had seen a vision of angels who said he was alive. Some of those who were with us went to the tomb and found it just as the women had said, but they didn't see him." (Luke 24:19–24)

Now, it looks like they had their facts right, so the way Jesus responds next might come as a surprise.

> He said to them, "How foolish and slow you are to believe all that the prophets have spoken! Wasn't it necessary for the Messiah to suffer

these things and enter into his glory?" (Luke 24:25–26)

Foolish and slow. This seems like a strong response from Jesus, doesn't it? Perhaps even harsh. Why did Jesus respond this way?

The two disciples already knew all they needed to know—they experienced all they needed to experience—yet they failed to connect the dots. They had the facts, but they were missing the obvious conclusion. Notice they reported that others said Jesus was alive and that no one could find the body in the tomb. However, they stopped short of saying that Jesus had risen.

This is why they were foolish. They were too slow of heart to put the pieces together and believe. They knew what the prophets had said. They saw what had happened the week before, and there's a good chance they had heard Jesus talk about His death and resurrection during the final part of His earthly ministry.

While Jesus' initial response seemed strong, what He did next reminds us of His kindness and graciousness. He walked the two travelers through the entire Old Testament, showing them how it all points to Him. Every single story. It's all part of one bigger story, the story of Jesus:

Then beginning with Moses and all the Prophets, he interpreted for them the things concerning himself in all the Scriptures. (Luke 24:27)

Luke 24:27 is a critical verse. That verse, along with verse 44 in the same chapter, serves as our interpretive key to the entire Bible. Jesus interpreted Scripture, not as a collection of random stories but as one big story about Him. We should do the same. Jesus is the connecting thread that ties all of Scripture together beautifully. Whenever we look at Scripture, our goal should be to look for Jesus. That is what the two disciples had missed. That is why they were foolish and slow. They knew the stories, but they didn't see *the story.*

Oh, to have been on the road that day listening in! Just imagine what it must have been like to hear Jesus teach through the Old Testament showing how it all connects to Him!

CHAPTER 8

SCATTERED STORIES AND SELF-IMPROVEMENT: HOW I LEARNED THE BIBLE

I grew up in the 1970s and '80s going to church every time the doors were open. This meant my family was at church on Sunday mornings, Sunday nights, and Wednesday nights. Rain, sleet, and snow couldn't keep us away. We were the post office of church attendees!

The churches we attended were good, Bible-believing churches. The church members loved God and believed the Bible was the inspired, inerrant Word of God. The pastors preached faithfully from the Bible week in and week out. The Sunday School teachers consistently taught from the Bible. There were Bibles everywhere you turned. Scripture was central in everything we did, but there was a problem: I never learned the gospel.

Now this isn't to say I never heard a gospel *presentation*—these were given at Vacation Bible School, on Easter, and during a few other times of the year. I heard I was a sinner, that Jesus died to pay the sin penalty, and that if I believed in Jesus, I would be saved. I heard these truths and responded to that gospel message when I was in the third grade.

However, I was just like the two disciples on the Emmaus Road. I had no idea that the Bible was one big story of Jesus. I thought the Old Testament's purpose was to help me understand who God is and how to live in a way that pleases Him (or to be more accurate, in a way to keep me out of trouble). I was aware of the Messianic prophecies, but I didn't think they were central to the main point of the Old Testament. These prophecies seemed to me merely to be "coming soon" teaser messages meant to connect the Old Testament with the New.

As a result, I grew up as a legalist—a little Pharisee. I believed that I had to live a certain way to please God and earn His love and acceptance. Oh, I knew that God loved me, but I had to act a certain way for Him to *really* love me. Basically, I lived my life believing that God was pleased with me based on what I did, not on who I was in Christ.

But I also knew that I wasn't really good at the whole "obeying God" thing. I was torn because I knew I should live one way, but deep down, I really wanted to live another way. My solution wasn't very innovative—I decided to live two different lives. I would live one way when I was at church or spending time with church friends and a different way when I was at school or hanging out with my unchurched friends.

From the world's eyes, I was a good kid, no matter which way I was living.

It wasn't too much of a leap then when I stopped attending church my freshman year in college. I didn't do anything crazy, but it was simply too easy to stay up late playing Super Mario Bros on Saturday nights and sleep until noon on Sundays. God was far off my radar. I never stopped believing in Him. I just stopped caring.

Remember, I grew up in good, Bible-believing churches! But like so many churches, the Bible was taught as isolated stories. My teachers and pastors took a moralistic approach to what we studied, especially when it came to the Old Testament. What else do you do with Joseph in Potiphar's house but conclude that the point of the story is that we need to resist sin? Where else can you go with the story of Moses than to say that working hard for God is what matters, even when it doesn't make sense on the surface? How else can you connect Jonah to modern life than to warn against the dangers of running from God?

That was how I learned the Bible. "Do this to please God. Don't do that because it will make God sad." Each Sunday added another do or don't item to my ever-growing mental list of what it took to please God.

All this time, I was never taught the one connecting thread of the Bible. I wasn't taught to look for Jesus in every story. Sadly, this is why I missed the gospel.

CHAPTER 9

THE GOSPEL: WHAT OUR KIDS REALLY NEED

Unfortunately, my story isn't uncommon. Maybe it's your story too. I tell you my story because I want to remind you (and me) of the need to focus our kids ministries on the gospel. When I was a child, I really wanted to follow God. I wanted to learn about Him and know Him. But without the connecting thread of Jesus, I was left hopeless and confused, just like the two disciples on the Emmaus Road. This is why I nearly gave up and became part of the 70 percent of young adults who walk away. The same thing can happen today to our kids if our ministries are not focused on the gospel.

Events are great, but activity itself does not give life. Staying busy has never made anyone right with God. Moral behavior is great, but it does not give life. Acting morally and virtuously has never made anyone right with God. Knowing the Bible is great, but head knowledge detached from the heart does not give life. Look at where that got the Emmaus disciples (and me)!

The gospel alone is what gives our kids life, hope, peace, and joy. Only the gospel satisfies our innermost longings. Only the gospel will transform our kids' hearts and lives. This is why we must never stray from the gospel—not even for one day. The gospel isn't just what we share to help kids come into saving

> **The gospel alone is what gives our kids life, hope, peace, and joy.**

faith; it must be the essence of everything we teach—every single time we teach. J.D. Greear puts it this way:

> *For many evangelicals the gospel has functioned solely as the entry rite into Christianity; it is the prayer we pray to begin our relationship with Jesus; the diving board off of which we jump into the pool of Christianity. After we get into the pool, we get into the real stuff of Christianity . . .*
>
> *The gospel, however, is not just the diving board off of which we jump into the pool of Christianity; it is the pool itself.*[3]

Because the gospel is what the Bible and discipleship is all about, we can never move past it. We never outgrow it. We can

---

3. J.D. Greear, *Gospel* (Nashville: B&H, 2011), 21.

never move on. I am reminded of this every time I read the book of Jude. After a brief greeting, this is how Jude opens his letter:

> **Dear friends, although I was eager to write you about the salvation we share, I found it necessary to write, appealing to you to contend for the faith that was delivered to the saints once for all. For some people, who were designated for this judgment long ago, have come in by stealth; they are ungodly, turning the grace of our God into sensuality and denying Jesus Christ, our only Master and Lord. (Jude 3–4)**

Jude had intended to explore some deeper issues of the faith with the early church, but after he heard that some men had entered the church and were leading it astray, he realized he needed to encourage the early church to contend for the faith by fighting for the gospel. Jude wanted the church to keep the gospel central. Doing so would protect them from false teachings, which had entered their community.

When I think of how Jude saw the gospel, I think of concentric circles similar to layers of an onion. The gospel in its most basic form is at the core.[4] Every layer moving out from that still connects to the gospel but amplifies it—that is why Jude still classified the deeper things he wanted to write about as the "salvation we share." It is all connected with the gospel at the center. Jude wanted to talk about some of those outer layers, but he felt the need to encourage the church to fight to protect the gospel at the very core instead. If the core falls apart, all the outer layers do too.

---

4. 1 Corinthians 15:1–8.

And that is why *everything* we do must be anchored to the gospel. Parents need to practice gospel-centered ministry. Kids leaders need to practice gospel-centered ministry. Kids need to experience gospel-centered ministry. And it begins largely with what we teach our kids.

CHAPTER 10

THE MYTH OF KIDS' BIBLE STORIES

Think about the Bible stories we most often tell our kids. There's Adam and Eve. Noah and the ark. Moses and the Exodus. Joshua and the battle of Jericho. Gideon. Samson. David and Goliath. Jonah. Daniel and the lions' den. Jesus' birth. The prodigal son. The Samaritan woman. David and Bathsheba. Wait, definitely not that one, right? That one is far too explicit for our kids. Cain and Abel? Nope. Not that one either. Too violent.

And this brings up the first problem. The idea that there are "kid stories" and then "adult stories" is just not biblical. Instead 2 Timothy 3:16 says that *all* Scripture is profitable. Note, it doesn't say *much* of Scripture, or even *most* Scripture. No, all Scripture is profitable regardless of its content!

And that takes us to the second problem—the criteria used to determine what's not a "kid's story." Sex and violence are usually the culprits here. Now, let me be clear; we certainly need to consider age-appropriateness in the manner by which we tell kids a Bible story. But let's think about this for a minute . . .

The creation story involving Adam and Eve centers on the couple being naked and unashamed and being commanded by God to populate the earth.[5] Yet Adam and Eve is a "kids' story," while David's sin with Bathsheba is not.

David and Goliath centers on David striking down Goliath and cutting off his head. Yet that story is considered a favorite "kids' story," while Cain murdering Abel is considered too violent.

The story of Noah and the ark features the entire world's population drowning except for one family. The account of Moses and the Exodus includes the murder of thousands of babies and Moses' killing an Egyptian in cold blood. Joshua and the battle of Jericho centers on an entire city being overthrown in battle. Gideon centers on another major battle.

Samson couldn't control his attraction to women, was violent and temperamental, and ended his life by dropping a house on top of himself and a number of Philistines. Jonah features God's prophet sitting on a hill, praying and waiting for God to wipe out all of the people in Nineveh. Daniel and the lions' den centers on Daniel being thrown to hungry lions, being protected by God, and then watching as his accusers and their families were thrown in and devoured.

---

5. Genesis 1:28; 2:24–25.

The story of Jesus' childhood includes the murder of little children. The prodigal son includes licentious living in a distant land. The Samaritan woman was a repeat adulteress.

So let me ask—what makes any of these "kid stories"? Why does violence in Cain and Abel make that story unacceptable for kids, while the violence in David and Goliath does not? Why does sex in David and Bathsheba make that story unacceptable for kids, while the command to multiply in Adam and Eve's story does not?

In most cases, the answer to these questions is found in how we tend to sanitize the stories we want to share with kids. When we teach on Noah and the ark, we focus on Noah and his family in the ark, but we simply ignore all of the people drowning outside of the ark. We paint Noah, his family, and the smiling animals on our preschool walls, but we leave off the screaming, drowning people in the water. (By the way, have you ever thought about that? Perhaps the most popular preschool decor happens to also be one of the most gruesome stories in the entire Bible!)

Without talking about death in Noah and the ark, we are left with just a story of Noah obeying God. This is important of course, but that is not the main point God wants us to walk away with from the story. God wants us to see the gospel in the Flood account. Noah and everyone else deserved to die because they were sinners. However, God extended grace to Noah and provided a way for him to be saved. Similarly, we deserve death for our sin, but God extends grace to us and provides a way for us to be saved in Jesus.

God did not design Bible stories to always be pleasant and entertaining for our kids. They are not intended to always make kids smile and say, "Well, that sure was a nice story!" Rather, every story in the Bible is designed to either proclaim or point toward the gospel in some way. This includes all the gospel, not just the "pleasant" parts of it. This is why so many Bible stories feature themes such as sin, death, and judgment. We cannot properly understand the more palatable parts of the gospel, such as God's love, grace, mercy, and forgiveness, apart from understanding our depravity and God's holiness.

We may find it difficult to teach the Bible the way God intends, that is, through the lens of the gospel. We often find it uncomfortable to talk to kids about topics that involve sin and death. This is why we tend to share "safe" passages and skip the "hard" ones. We need to resist this tendency and faithfully teach God's Word to our kids. That said, we must determine what is age appropriate—especially for pre-schoolers and younger elementary kids. We can mention sin and death without expounding on the gory, bloody, explicit details.

> God did not design Bible stories to always be pleasant and entertaining for our kids.

We teach our kids what the Bible says about sin, evil, violence, and death so that we can give them hope. They need to know that they don't have to be afraid of these things because Jesus defeated darkness two thousand years ago when He died on a cross and walked out of a tomb. Our kids don't have to fear death because Jesus defeated it! Our kids don't have to despair in sin because Jesus was victorious in their place.

Do you still have reservations about teaching kids the unpleasant parts of the Bible? Let's look for a moment at Deuteronomy 6:4–9. This classic passage shares God's plan for how parents are to disciple their kids. At the center of the passage is God's instruction that parents are to talk about God's Word with their kids all the time. Parents are called to weave God's Word into their normal rhythms of life.

Now, when we teach this passage today, we often make the mistake of reading our own New Testament context into the passage. We equate talking about God's Word with our kids with talking about Jesus, God's love, and all the other "good parts" of the Bible. But what did God intend for Israel to do when He originally gave them this command? What did these Old Testament parents have to share with their kids?

These parents only had the first five books of the Old Testament—the Torah. Think about the Bible stories included in these books. Most are "hard" stories, stories of sin and violence. Parents were called to talk about these themes with their kids deeply, not superficially.

And this takes us to the third problem with kids' Bible stories. If we water down Bible stories, what are we left with? What are we teaching our kids? How are we teaching them to read and understand the Bible?

Whatever we are left with, it is not the gospel. At least, it's not the gospel in its full power and splendor. If we withhold the gospel from our kids, we run the risk of raising modern-day Emmaus Road disciples. These kids may grow up to understand parts of the Bible but will likely miss Who it's all about—Jesus.

This is what we've done in so many churches today. It's why so many young adults are walking away from the church. We've failed to give kids the gospel. We failed to do what was needed because it was too hard and made us uncomfortable. Our kids have paid the consequences.

We cannot afford to neglect the gospel any longer. We have to do what it takes—whatever it takes—to share the full gospel with our kids. Failure is not an option. We need to reject the notion of *kids' stories* and do the hard work of teaching *Bible stories* in age-appropriate ways.

CHAPTER 11

IT'S ALWAYS DARKEST BEFORE THE DAWN: WHY WE NEED THE GOSPEL

Before we can teach our kids the gospel, we need to make sure we have a firm grasp of the gospel ourselves. I don't mean a brief gospel outline, such as what is found in an evangelistic tract (although tools like this can be helpful and certainly have a place). I mean the grand narrative of redemption woven throughout the entire Bible. The story of the gospel. The story of Jesus.

Our kids need to understand the entire gospel story. The gospel story gives meaning and context for everything in the Bible. The gospel story reveals the heart of God. The gospel story encourages kids to trust in Christ and enter into His story.

Let's step back and look at the story of the Bible from a high vantage point. We begin on a positive note, but as we will see, the story quickly takes a dark turn.

Chapter 1: God Created

The story begins, at least from our perspective, with creation. But for us to really understand the gospel story, we have to understand *why* God created, not just know *that* He created. Psalm 19:1–3 is a good place to begin:

> **The heavens declare the glory of God, and the expanse proclaims the work of his hands. Day after day they pour out speech; night after night they communicate knowledge. There is no speech; there are no words; their voice is not heard.**

Creation has a chief purpose. Everything exists to reveal the glory of God. The Creator is always greater than creation. This is why the amazing expanse of the universe enables us to better appreciate God's omnipresence. When we think of the power of something like our sun—a relatively modest star in relation to the rest of the universe—it

> Creation has a chief purpose. Everything exists to reveal the glory of God. The Creator is always greater than creation.

enables us to better appreciate God's omnipotence. When we think of the beauty of Earth, it enables us to better appreciate God's beauty and creativity.

As created beings, people share in the same purpose of bringing glory to God. Indeed, this is what happened for however long it took the story of Genesis 1 and 2 to unfold. But then, Genesis 3 came, and with it, the next chapter of the big story was revealed.

Chapter 2: Man Rebelled

All it took was one act of sin for God's creation to fall apart. Satan took on the form of a serpent and tricked Eve to disobey God and eat of the Tree of the Knowledge of Good and Evil. Adam, who was with her, ate also. Everything changed in that instant. The uninvited guest of death entered into creation. Adam and Eve's unity and intimacy were broken. The ground rebelled against Adam's work. Childbirth became painful. And worst of all, humankind's relationship with God was broken.

> Adam and Eve were deceived into thinking that God owed them and that He was unjust to withhold certain pleasures.

We often think of the first sin as Adam and Eve eating the fruit, but it actually started before that. It began in the heart, when Adam and Eve refused to believe God's goodness and truthfulness. Sin was present when Adam and Eve believed they were entitled to more than what God had provided. They were deceived into thinking that God owed them and that He was unjust to withhold certain pleasures. Sin was running wild when Adam and Eve desired to be like God in trying to exert their own sovereignty. Creation wanted to be Creator. It was at this point that sin manifested into the physical act of eating from the tree. If we only focus on the moment when Adam and Eve physically ate of the tree, we miss the heart issues behind the act. This is what sin is really all about.

And that is what our kids need to know about sin. The battle of sin is won and lost in the heart. Apart from Jesus, we will lose every single time. That's why Jesus focused on the heart in the Sermon on the Mount. The heart is the breeding ground for sin, and that is where we can either fertilize it in the flesh or use the pesticide of the gospel.

> **If we only focus on the moment when Adam and Eve physically ate of the tree, we miss the heart issues behind the act. This is what sin is really all about.**

Death. Broken relationship with God. Broken relationships with others. Struggle to find purpose in life. These are the same consequences that continue to plague humanity today because all have sinned and face sin's repercussions.[6]

Just like that, the beauty of the story's first act was overshadowed by darkness. As bleak as the story is at this point, it gets even worse before it gets better. But we have to go where the story takes us, and we have to take our kids there too.

---

6. Romans 3:23; 6:23.

Chapter 3: Man Tried to Make Things Right

When we think of the gospel, we normally move straight from man's sin to the provision of Jesus. However, the Bible doesn't move directly from Genesis 3 to Matthew 1 (although that would make our read-through-the-Bible-in-a-year plans much easier to follow!). Instead, everything in Genesis 4 through Malachi 4 points to the gospel. Our goal is to understand how this works.

Perhaps it will help if we think broadly about the Old Testament. When I think of the Old Testament, one word comes quickly to mind—failure. Think about all the times we see God's people fail miserably in the Old Testament. Pick any person—even the "stars" like Abraham, Moses, and David—and you'll see a person who sinned grievously against God. Abraham lied twice in saying Sarah was not his wife to protect his own neck. Moses killed a man. David committed adultery and murder.

Now think about how God's people as a whole repeatedly walked—or ran—away from God and committed idolatry. Consider how God's people broke the law, ignored God's warnings, demanded a king, and treated each other unjustly.

The Old Testament clearly shows the depth of sin and people's complete inability to do anything about it. Some people thought they could be good enough to please God. That didn't work. Others thought they could be religious enough to please God. That didn't work. Some people assumed their ethnicity (their Jewish heritage) was enough to please God. Alas, that didn't work either.

Nothing worked because there is nothing we can do to overcome sin.[7] The Old Testament screams of the need for a salvation that comes from outside of us.[8] This is where we're reminded of God's love, grace, mercy, and beauty. As we read about humanity's failures on page after page of the Old Testament, we also begin to discover God's ongoing plan to provide the answer in Jesus. Salvation was possible and was on its way. The beauty of the gospel is that it would not be based off of human effort; rather, it would rest entirely on what God would do on humanity's behalf.

> As we read about humanity's failures on page after page of the Old Testament, we also begin to discover God's ongoing plan to provide the answer in Jesus.

7. Galatians 3:24.
8. Ephesians 2:8–9.

CHAPTER 12

BEAUTY FROM ASHES: THE HOPE OF THE GOSPEL

After the first two glorious chapters of Genesis, the third chapter brings devastating news. Adam and Eve rebelled against God and plunged all of humanity into sin, death, and hopelessness. From this point on in the Bible, nothing provides deliverance from sin. Nothing provides life. Nothing makes us right with God again. Well, nothing that mere man can do.

Chapter 4: God Provided Jesus

All this did not catch God off guard. Even before creation, God had a plan to provide rescue for His people. This rescue would come from God Himself. There was hope. Hope from God. Hope that would be realized in Jesus.

God had warned Adam and Eve that if they disobeyed Him, they would die. Some may think that death is a pretty extreme punishment for eating a piece of fruit, but we have to remember that the weight of sin is not measured by the act itself as much as by the One against whom sin is committed. And all sin is against a perfectly holy and pure God.[9] This is why the wages of sin—all sin—is death.[10]

Death was owed, and a death was paid through the sacrifice of Jesus.[11] However, before there was death, there was the most amazing birth of all time. The birth of Jesus—God in the flesh. Jesus lived a sinless life of perfect obedience to the Father, was crucified and died to pay the sin penalty He did not deserve. He then rose from the dead, signifying that death and sin had been defeated once and for all.

This is the central message of the four Gospels and is the story that all of Scripture revolves around. In God's wisdom, love, kindness, and grace, He settled the sin problem we could not solve. He gave us Jesus to die in our place.

This doctrine of Jesus dying in our place, also known as substitutionary atonement, is taught clearly in the Bible,[12] most notably in Romans 5:6–11. After writing about the pervasive sin problem we all face in the first three chapters of Romans, Paul turned his attention to the one and only solution of Jesus. By the time Paul got to chapter 5, he was deep in awe of this beautiful doctrine:

---

9. Romans 3:23.
10. Romans 6:23.
11. Hebrews 9:22.
12. Ephesians 1:7-10; Colossians 1:19–20.

For while we were still helpless, at the right time, Christ died for the ungodly. For rarely will someone die for a just person — though for a good person perhaps someone might even dare to die. But God proves his own love for us in that while we were still sinners, Christ died for us. How much more then, since we have now been declared righteous by his blood, will we be saved through him from wrath. For if, while we were enemies, we were reconciled to God through the death of his Son, then how much more, having been reconciled, will we be saved by his life. And not only that, but we also rejoice in God through our Lord Jesus Christ, through whom we have now received this reconciliation. (Rom. 5:6–11)

Notice how Paul describes who we were apart from Christ. We were weak, ungodly, sin-stricken enemies of God. We were weak because we were powerless to do anything about our sin condition. We were ungodly because we chose to turn away from God in rebellion. We were sinners by nature. The fruit coming out of our life was rotten to the core. And perhaps most sobering, we were enemies of God, operating in open warfare against our Creator.

It isn't popular to describe people like this today. Instead, our culture likes to say that people are basically good. This perspective has even seeped into the church. It's a worldview which says that people—especially kids—are good at the core and that they just need a little help to make them right with God again. "We aren't dead in sin," they say, "We're just a little under the weather." But as we see, that isn't what the Bible teaches. No, if we want fully to experience the majesty of the gospel, we have to go to the deepest, darkest places of our hearts and repent. We have to wrap our arms around how evil and wicked we were before Jesus saved us. This honest assessment of our desperate condition allows us to see the amazing beauty of God's love for us in the form of the substitutionary atonement.

As sinful as we were, God stepped into our sad state and justified us through the blood of Christ. Because Jesus paid our sin penalty, we can be perfectly right with God again with absolutely no barrier between us. We can be saved from God's wrath and can be reconciled to Him as adopted children. When we think of who we were apart from Christ and what He has done for us, it's hard to imagine it getting any better. But it does!

When most people think of the gospel, they think of a one-way transaction—basically what we have talked about to this point—the substitutionary atonement. But the gospel is actually a two-way transaction. Jesus took our sin from us and put it on Himself, but He also placed something of His own on us: His perfection.

Let this sink in. Jesus was sinless, yet He took all of our sin and put it on Himself and died for us, while simultaneously giving us the credit for His perfect obedience to the Father. He got our sin; we got His perfection. Paul beautifully encapsulates this in 2 Corinthians 5:21:

> **He made the one who did not know sin to be sin for us, so that in him we might become the righteousness of God.**

At least that is true for those who have trusted in Christ. There is nothing we can do to earn salvation. Neither is there anything we can do to maintain salvation. Salvation is a free gift of God, but it does require faith in Jesus.[13] J.D. Greear explains, "The gospel is an announcement that Jesus is Lord and that He has won the battle for your salvation. We are to respond in repentance and faith (Mark 1:15). The gospel is not *good advice* about how to live; it is good news about what God has done."[14]

Although this is certainly good news, it's not where the gospel ends. After Jesus ascends to the Father at the beginning of Acts, there are another twenty-three books left in the New Testament. The rest of the good news of the gospel takes us to the next two chapters. In them, we'll learn what our lives should now look like because of the gospel and we'll discover what our lives will look like for eternity.

Chapter 5: Jesus Changes His People

The Book of Acts is sometimes also called Acts of the Apostles. That's a helpful clarification, but I'm with those who favor referring to it as Acts of the Holy Spirit instead. Acts of the Apostles puts the emphasis on people, while Acts of the Holy Spirit emphasizes the Holy Spirit's vital role in forming the early church. Without the work of the Holy Spirit transforming the early believers day-by-day, the Book of Acts wouldn't exist. It wasn't Peter and Paul who turned the world upside down; it was the Holy Spirit working through them.

---

13. Romans 10:13–17; Ephesians 2:8–9.
14. Greear, *Gospel*, 222

This work of the Holy Spirit is what we experience in the book of Acts and in the Epistles. God was showing the early church what it looked like for them to be changed into the image of Jesus as they lived out the gospel in their context. Whereas legalism encourages people to attempt to please God through their own efforts (something that can't be done!), we see the early church pleasing God in the Spirit's power by learning to trust in the finished work of Christ.

We also see how the early church drew their motivations from the gospel. They were not motivated by the need to please God or be accepted by Him. They knew they already fully pleased God and were accepted by Him because they had been given Christ's righteousness. They were motivated by loving gratitude and awe of the goodness of God. This motivation, partnered with the power of the Holy Spirit, began a gospel revolution.

Chapter 6: Jesus Will Make All Things Right Again

That almost wraps up the gospel story in the Bible. Almost. There's still additional good news that comes mostly from the book of Revelation. One day Jesus will make everything right again, and sin and death will be no more.

When we think of the gospel, and many of the Bible's promises, we have to think in terms of two categories—"already" and "not yet." There are certain aspects of the gospel—of salvation—that are already true. We are already completely forgiven in Christ. We are already seen as righteous by God. We are already given eternal life.

But at the same time, there are other aspects of the gospel we do not yet experience. While we are fully forgiven in

Christ and seen as righteous by God, we continue to struggle with sin. While we are given eternal life, we will still die physically.

The book of Revelation says when Jesus returns He will merge the already and the not-yet promises of God. Sin will be completely done away with forever. Death will be no more. God's people will once again worship, serve, and know God as He intended in Eden. Jesus has already won the total victory, but on that Day we will experience the fullness of His victory.

Our kids need the hope of Christ's return to help them live victoriously, joyfully, and intentionally. The only way for them to grasp this hope is by walking through the previous five chapters of the gospel story. That is why our kids need gospel-centered teaching.

Questions for Reflection and Discussion

- Did you learn the Bible as a collection of stories or as one big story about God and His plan to redeem a people for Himself? How does your experience impact your understanding of the gospel today?
- Which parts of the gospel are most challenging for you? Why?
- Does the curriculum your kids ministry uses point to Jesus in every session? If not, how can you make sure that happens?
- Do you have an intentional plan for teaching preschoolers and children in your ministry from birth through the preteen years?

- What are some of the challenges of gospel-centered teaching in preschool and kids ministry? What are some of the rewards?
- Which stories are most difficult for you to teach? Why? What can you do to overcome this and teach them faithfully?

Application: Gospel-Centered Teaching

1. **Develop a curriculum evaluation tool.** Evaluate your primary Bible study curriculum, as well as potential curriculum for Vacation Bible School, camps, retreats, etc. Consider including the following evaluators:

- What is the publisher's and curriculum's stated philosophy and purpose?
- What stories are covered? What stories are not covered? Why?
- Who is the hero of the story being told each week?
- How many times is Jesus mentioned in a typical session?
- How often is sin mentioned and how is it defined?
- What type of application is given? Is it built on the gospel or on moralism?
- Is there a family connection to help you partner with families in their discipleship role?

2. **Develop and conduct a gospel-centered teaching training session.** Use the ideas from this book and other

resources to develop a training session for all those who serve in kids ministry—not just classroom teachers. Consider making attendance a requirement to serve in kids ministry to affirm your church's and ministry's value of gospel centrality. If you do this, think about recording the session on video for those who cannot make the live training.

–PART 3–

GOSPEL-CENTERED

TRANSFORMATION

CHAPTER 13

TELL US MORE: FINDING BEAUTY IN THE GOSPEL

The two travelers on the road to Emmaus had heard Jesus explain the Old Testament to them in a way they had never experienced before. For the first time, they saw how each story of the Old Testament connected as part of the one big story of Jesus and His gospel. Thus, it was not surprising that they pleaded with Jesus to stay with them as they concluded their journey. They wanted more.

They came near the village where they were going, and he gave the impression that he was going farther. But they urged him, "Stay with us, because it's almost evening, and now the day is

**almost over." So he went in to stay with them. It
was as he reclined at the table with them that he
took the bread, blessed and broke it, and gave
it to them. Then their eyes were opened, and
they recognized him, but he disappeared from
their sight. They said to each other, "Weren't our
hearts burning within us while he was talking
with us on the road and explaining the Scriptures
to us?" (Luke 24:28–32)**

We can only guess at what it was about Jesus' breaking the bread and blessing it that caused their eyes to be
opened. Perhaps it was a unique way Jesus broke the bread.
Or perhaps it was what He said as He blessed it. Did He
repeat what He had told the disciples at the Last Supper?
Or perhaps it was simply an act of God. Whatever it was,
the two finally recognized Jesus in the flesh—much like they
finally recognized Jesus in the words of the Old Testament.

Then, Jesus vanished from their sight. However, He
didn't leave them entirely. Christ's words echoed in their
minds and hearts. As they heard the story of Jesus—the
gospel—explained as one story woven throughout the
Bible, their hearts burned within them. Their affections
were stirred. And it's no wonder. God has hardwired us to
crave Christ as He's revealed through the gospel, whether we
realize it or not. The gospel's presentation of Jesus is the only
thing that quenches the thirst of our souls.

It wasn't the stories that stoked the fires of their hearts—
they knew the stories. It was the connecting thread of
Jesus—what they had missed up to this point—that moved
them so deeply and profoundly.

We should long for our kids to experience the gospel in this manner—in such a way that it moves them deeply and changes them forever. It begins with how we help kids apply the Bible to their lives.

CHAPTER 14

BE LIKE DAVID: MORALISTIC APPLICATION

Let's take a minute and consider how one of the most well-known Bible stories in the Old Testament—David and Goliath in 1 Samuel 17—is often taught and applied.

The story opens with the Philistine and Israelite armies at a stalemate. The two opposing armies were encamped on hills separated by a ravine. Whichever army left its position to attack the other would have been at a distinct disadvantage. It's likely this was why the two armies were at a standstill.

Every morning and evening for forty days, Goliath, the enormous nine-foot, nine-inch Philistine champion, would make his way into the ravine between the two armies and invite one Israelite to face him in battle. Whichever man won would win the battle for his nation. Day after day,

Goliath made the same offer. And day after day, the Israelites trembled in fear. No one went out to face Goliath. To do so would have been suicide. Goliath was an unbeatable enemy.

About this time, David's father, Jesse, sent his young son to visit his brothers and take them some provisions. When David arrived, he witnessed one of Goliath's daily taunts and saw that no Israelite soldier would face the giant. David couldn't believe this, so he went to King Saul and volunteered to fight Goliath. Saul tried to dissuade him at first, pointing out that David was a youth—most likely a teenager—and that Goliath was an experienced warrior. David persisted, so Saul finally consented. David put on Saul's armor, but it didn't fit so he took it off. Then, armed only with his sling, his staff, and a few stones, he went out to face Goliath.

Goliath must have been excited to finally receive an opponent. That is, until he got a better view of David and realized he was a puny teenager. Goliath unleashed a fury of taunts, but David was resolute. David told Goliath he would kill him that day by the power of God. Then, he ran at the giant.

Then David took one stone, loaded it into the sling, and unleashed it at his foe. The stone struck Goliath in the forehead and he fell over. David ran to the fallen giant, took the Philistine's sword, and used it to cut off

> **David was resolute. David told Goliath he would kill him that day by the power of God. Then, he ran at the giant.**

his head. The battle was won. When the Philistines saw what happened, they ran in fear and the Israelites routed them.

Now comes the application, or misapplication. Many of us were taught that David was brave because he trusted in God, and God blessed his faith with a victory over Goliath. We also were told that there are giants in our lives and we need to be like David and be brave as we trust God for victory.

There's a problem with that application, though. Where's Jesus? And who can actually live up to that application? Sure, being brave sounds great on paper, but how many of us actually can be brave on the level David was? When we teach the Bible like this, we rob it of its power—the gospel—and we set our kids up for failure and frustration. There's a better way.

> **When we teach the Bible like this, we rob it of its power—the gospel—and we set our kids up for failure and frustration. There's a better way.**

CHAPTER 15

LOOK AT JESUS: GOSPEL APPLICATION

Let's take a step back and look more broadly at the story of David and Goliath. The essence of the story is that an unlikely hero defeats a seemingly unbeatable enemy. No one thought that Goliath could be defeated, certainly not at the hands of a young boy with a few rocks for weapons. Yet, David did what was completely unexpected; he defeated Goliath, and did so in convincing fashion. This is a picture of the gospel.

Jesus is the greater David. Jesus was the unlikely hero who defeated the seemingly unbeatable enemy of sin and death. David was offered King Saul's armor and weapons—military equipment that was expected in battle—but he rejected it and instead faced Goliath in an unexpected way.

In a similar way, most Israelites expected Jesus to bring them deliverance from their earthly enemies through a show of political or military force. However, Jesus rejected their plans for Him and delivered them in an unexpected way from their true enemies: sin, death, and God's wrath. Just as David was resolute in facing Goliath and ran toward him in battle, Jesus was resolute in facing sin and death and traveled to Jerusalem to go to battle on a cross.[15]

David defeated Goliath in convincing fashion. It took him only one stone to strike down the enemy. And then, so that no one would doubt the victory, David cut off Goliath's head showing everyone—God's people and their enemies alike—that the battle was won for God's glory. Jesus defeated sin and death in convincing fashion. He struck down sin and death on the cross, and then, so that no one would doubt the victory, He arose on the third day to show everyone—God's people and their enemies—that the battle was won for God's glory.

That is what God wants us to see in this story, and that is what we need to teach our kids. As we teach this Bible story, our kids need to understand that David and Goliath were real and part of redemptive history. We need to honor this story in its immediate context. However, we cannot teach it in isolation of the big story of Jesus. We need to connect what we see in David and Goliath to the gospel; that is the only way we will reach proper gospel-centered application.

When we show kids how David is the precursor to Jesus, we give them an opportunity to see more of the beauty and power behind the gospel. The story of David defeating a

---

15. Luke 9:51.

giant won't stir our affections like the story of Jesus defeating sin and death will. This focus, a gospel-focus, gives us the context we need to teach kids about bravery.

There is nothing wrong with encouraging our kids to be brave in light of David and Goliath—if we do it the right way. We don't tell them to emulate David and be brave in life as they face giants. That's teaching moralism. Instead, we tell kids they can be brave in life no matter what because Jesus has already defeated their greatest enemies: sin and death! If God defeated that seemingly unbeatable enemy, what do we have left to fear? No matter what happens on Earth, if we trust in Jesus' victory, we can know sin and death have no power over us. The battle is won! Jesus is the victor and He has shared that victory with us.

> **When we show kids how David is the precursor to Jesus, we give them an opportunity to see more of the beauty and power behind the gospel.**

CHAPTER 16

OBEDIENCE FOR OR OBEDIENCE FROM: HOW THE GOSPEL CHANGES US

When we force immediate application out of passages at the expense of understanding its place in the gospel narrative, we end up with moralism. We tell kids to be brave like David. We focus on what we are to do instead of what Jesus has already done. We find our worth in our actions for God instead of our identity in Christ. None of that brings life. None of that brings joy. None of that brings God glory.

However, when we teach the Bible through a gospel lens, we position our kids to receive a beautiful, lasting gospel transformation. Our target is a transformed heart, not changed behavior. A transformed heart will always result in changed behavior that honors God, but changed behavior will not always result in a transformed heart that yields to God.

J.D. Greear puts it this way, "We are changed not by being told what we need to do for God, but by hearing the news about what God has done for us."[16]

It is critical that we understand this and frame our Bible teaching, especially our application, around it. We cannot move straight to application through bypassing the gospel. We need to filter everything we teach through the gospel and present the riches of Jesus to our kids week-in and week-out as we pray for God to transform their hearts.

Should we ever tell kids what they should do? Certainly! The Bible is full of imperatives. We cannot be bashful when it comes to declaring that which God has clearly said. But we always follow the "what" of God's commands with the "why." And that "why" is always anchored to the gospel in looking at who Jesus is and what He has done. We want our kids to love Jesus so deeply that they desire to obey God's commands as a byproduct of that love. They obey out of gratitude, not obligation. They obey with joy, not with resentment. They obey out of an overflowing appreciation of the gospel.

Think of how the New Testament Epistles follow this blueprint. Let's look at Romans as an example. Romans 1–11 is Paul's masterful treatise of the gospel. In these 11 chapters of rich theology, Paul explains our desperate sinful state and offers the wonderful answer for our condition—the substitutionary atonement of Jesus. There aren't many imperatives in this section of Romans. Instead the focus is on who God is

---

16. Greear, *Gospel*. 64.

and what He has done through Jesus Christ. Then we reach Romans 12–16, which is replete with imperatives instructing us how to live as new creatures in Christ.

The hinge between these two sections begins with, "Therefore, brothers and sisters, in view of the mercies of God, I urge you . . ." (Rom.12:1). The connection is clear. Therefore—because of all that has preceded this—namely Romans 1–11, the gospel—here is how you are to live. How we are to live follows what we understand about the gospel. The gospel is true and beautiful; therefore, our lives should be transformed. That is the blueprint of the Epistles. Our understanding of God should always precede an application of how we ought to live.

The reason why we are to live out the gospel is beautiful. How we are to live out the gospel may be even more amazing. Paul gives us a glimpse of this in his letter to the church at Philippi.

> **Therefore, my dear friends, just as you have always obeyed, so now, not only in my presence but even more in my absence, work out your own salvation with fear and trembling. For it is God who is working in you both to will and to work according to his good purpose. Do everything without grumbling and arguing, so that you may be blameless and pure, children of God who are faultless in a crooked and perverted generation, among whom you shine like stars in the world. (Phil. 2:12–15)**

Notice that Paul tells the church they are to work out their salvation. He later tells them they are to work it out without grumbling and arguing. In other words, they are to do it with joy and gratitude. But notice also how God tells them they'll be able to grow—it will be God working in them. This is the stunner of the gospel.

God brings us into relationship with Him through His Son and calls on us to live for His glory. Then, He empowers us to carry out that command! Even what we are to do in proper response to the gospel is done through God's grace, mercy, and power. This is why no matter how deeply we familiarize ourselves with the gospel, we always find ourselves pointing to God's goodness and celebrating His work instead of our own achievements.

And this is how we need to teach our kids. Yes, obedience matters. We can't look past the imperatives of Scripture under the pretext of grace and freedom in Christ. In Christ, we are not free to live however we want. In Christ, we are finally free to live for God through His power! Obedience matters, not because it earns God's love, but because it testifies that the gospel has taken root in our hearts. Or as J.D. Greear puts it, "God motivates us from acceptance, not toward it."[17]

---

17. Greear, *Gospel*, 54.

CHAPTER 17

THE HOLLOW OBEDIENCE OF THE PHARISEES

When we read through the four Gospels, we see that the Pharisees struggled to understand that obedience should come from God's favor, not for God's favor.

The Pharisees were one of the two major Jewish groups in Jesus' day, with the other being the Sadducees. The Sadducees were more of a political power. They partnered closely with Rome and controlled most of the Sanhedrin—the ruling body in Israel. The Pharisees, meanwhile, were the people's party. They had more power and influence with the Jewish people than with Rome. They captured the respect and awe of the people by obeying the law as strictly as possible.

The Pharisees would strain out a gnat to keep from consuming even the smallest unclean creature. They would tithe the most minuscule amount, even giving from their spices. They wore every piece of religious apparel they could. They prayed lengthy prayers. When a common Jew looked at a Pharisee, everything he saw projected complete and total obedience to God. But how did Jesus feel about the obedience of the Pharisees? He rejected it—all of it.

Instead of praising the Pharisees as the people would have expected, Jesus declared woe on them. Instead of calling them the elites, He called them hypocrites. They were whitewashed tombs—clean and sparkling on the outside, but dead on the inside. You cannot read Jesus' strong condemnations toward the Pharisees in Matthew 23 without your jaw dropping. What Jesus says to the Pharisees seems, at first, so out of character. We are used to seeing Jesus as kind, gentle, loving, and patient with people, but here He strongly condemns the Pharisees. Why? Because the Pharisees obeyed God's law for all the wrong reasons.

The Pharisees weren't seeking to please God and honor Him through their obedience; they wanted to earn the praise of men and the acceptance of God on their own terms. Jesus addressed this kind of lifestyle in the strongest possible terms so that the people wouldn't be misled by the Pharisees' moralistic example.

Obedience doesn't save. God saves. Obedience detached from the gospel doesn't please. Christ's righteousness pleases. That is something I didn't begin learning until midway through college. Earlier in this book, I shared the story of how I learned the Bible as a collection of isolated, moral-based stories. I grew up as a modern "Pharisee" as a result.

By the time I was a freshman in college, I had practically given up on trying to be good enough. I still believed in

God. I just was tired of trying to please Him, and I had grown apathetic. I experienced the devastation of the soul that Matt Chandler and Jared Wilson talk about in their book *The Explicit Gospel.*

> *"For some reason—namely, our depravity—we have a tendency to think that the cross saves us from past sin, but after we are saved, we have to take over and clean ourselves up. This sort of thinking is devastating to the soul."*[18]

I had trusted in Jesus to save me years before, but I'd been trying to live life on my own power and against a standard I could never meet. It was a loss from the start, and I was ready to throw in the towel.

Then one day during my sophomore year, I was waiting in the cafeteria line (I still can't believe we lined up for that terrible food!), and someone asked me if I would complete a brief survey on an index card. I had nothing better to do, so I took a card and a pen and looked at the survey. It was a spiritual interest survey of just a few basic questions. I completed it along with my name and phone number and didn't give it much thought except that I had nailed it, being the "Pharisee" that I was.

A week or so later, a guy named Charlie called and asked if we could meet and talk about the survey. I didn't want to. Remember, I was a retired "Pharisee"—or at least a "Pharisee" on sabbatical. I really didn't have any desire to

---

18. Matt Chandler with Jared Wilson, *The Explicit Gospel* (Wheaton, IL: Crossway, 2012), 14.

talk about God, the Bible, or faith with someone, especially some stranger.

So while almost every fiber in me was saying no, one part said yes—my mouth. I could tell you that I was just too polite to say no, but the truth is that God was providentially at work. That one simple word would change my life, even if I wouldn't realize it for quite a while.

As it turns out, Charlie was on staff with Cru (Campus Crusade for Christ as it was known at the time), and this is what he did on a regular basis—connect with college students in an attempt to share the gospel. A few days later it was time for Charlie to come over and meet. I almost ducked out on him by intentionally being out of my room

> **That one simple word would change my life, even if I wouldn't realize it for quite a while.**

when it was time for us to get together, but again I was too nice—or better yet, God was still working providentially—so I didn't.

Charlie and I talked for about an hour that day, and it was tolerable. As the time was winding down, I remember thinking that I was almost free and clear of Charlie. I'd been polite and had honored our appointment. I could now move on with my pharisaical flunky life. But at the last minute, Charlie asked if we could meet again. And to my horror, I said yes.

Charlie and I began meeting on a regular basis that year, and you know what happened? In time, I actually began to look forward to our conversations. Unlike when I was a kid in church learning isolated Bible stories and their accompanying moralistic lessons, Charlie began to help me see the gospel. I began to understand who God is and to see His heart. I began to make sense of the Bible. Slowly. But it was progress all the same and as a result, my heart was starting to change. I was experiencing gospel-transformation.

By the end of my college career, God had taken me from being a washed-out "Pharisee" who didn't want to talk about God at all, to being a leader of a freshman Bible study, emcee at weekly Cru meetings, and a mission trip participant. God had begun to break me of my superficial, shallow attempt at being a "good Christian" on the outside. I had experienced heart-change, and my life would never be the same.

CHAPTER 18

THE GOSPEL IN THE SERMON ON THE MOUNT

While Jesus directly and strongly condemned the Pharisees when He talked with them, He usually took a different approach when He talked with the lay people of the day. Jesus actually used the Pharisees' example of spiritual showmanship to shatter the myth that God's acceptance comes through external obedience.

The average Jew assumed that the Pharisees were God's favorites—the star pupils moved to the front of the class. This is why the people were probably stunned when Jesus said, "For I tell you, unless your righteousness surpasses that of the scribes and Pharisees, you will never get into the kingdom of heaven" (Matt. 5:20). I can see the wide eyes and open mouths in the crowd. "We have to do what? Be better than the Pharisees!? There's no way! That's impossible!"

Most of the people probably wanted to throw up their hands in surrender at that moment. It was hopeless. "Can someone even be more righteous than the Pharisees?" they likely asked themselves. I imagine there were some people who actually thought about leaving Jesus at that point—kind of like what I did in college.

Perhaps this is why Jesus used this shocking statement toward the beginning of the Sermon on the Mount, rather than at the end. He was going to show them how they could indeed be more righteous than the Pharisees. What Jesus said next is the key to understanding what true righteousness consists of:

> **"You have heard that it was said to our ancestors, Do not murder, and whoever murders will be subject to judgment. But I tell you, everyone who is angry with his brother or sister will be subject to judgment. Whoever insults his brother or sister, will be subject to the court. Whoever says, 'You fool!' will be subject to hellfire." (Matt. 5:21–22)**

Notice that Jesus began by pointing the people to a way they could be obedient to God—in this case, by not murdering. He then contrasted that with a command of His own—in this case, not to be angry with someone else. Murder is something a person does, an act of the hands, but anger is a condition of the heart.

Do you see what Jesus was saying? The people thought that external behavior made a person righteous. Jesus wanted them to see that true righteousness is found in a person's heart. A person who doesn't murder, but who still hates, isn't righteous at all. But a righteous person who doesn't hate won't murder. Hate is the internal fuel for the external act of murder.

Focus on external behavior and you will miss the internal heart, but focus on the internal heart and you will get both. That is the key to righteousness. That is the central message of the Sermon on the Mount. And that is the key to gospel-centered transformation and application. Go to the heart, and the hands will follow.

Continue reading and you will see that Jesus uses the same formula for adultery and breaking oaths. Instead of starting with external behavior, He encourages us to start with the heart and let the external behavior follow naturally.

Don't focus only on the external act of adultery. Instead, focus on keeping lust out of your heart. Without lust, adultery won't happen. Don't focus only on the external act of breaking an oath. Instead, focus on keeping a heart of integrity. With integrity, broken oaths won't happen.

> Focus on external behavior and you will miss the internal heart, but focus on the internal heart and you will get both.

What the Pharisees and the people didn't understand is that God judges the heart, and a heart that is truly transformed by the gospel will bear fruit for a new way of life. That is why Jesus told the people that their righteousness had to surpass that of the Pharisees. The external behavior of the Pharisees was not righteousness; it was a facade covering hearts that were far from God.

We have to point our kids to the heart over and over again just like Jesus did in the Sermon on the Mount. The heart is where the battle is won or lost. When we allow the Holy Spirit to work the gospel deep down into our kids' hearts, it will show itself in what they do with their hands as well. This is the kind of gospel transformation we are after: Helping our kids trust in the gospel, finding acceptance from God based on Jesus taking their sin and giving them His righteousness, and living in obedience out of love and gratitude.

> **The heart is where the battle is won or lost.**

It's not about what you do; it's about who you are. And who you are is proven by what you do. That's the Sermon on the Mount in a nutshell.

CHAPTER 19

CHURCH: A COMMUNITY OF CHANGING PEOPLE

This is a good place to bring our discussion back to the state of the church. Gospel transformation is vital to understanding the nature of the church and the value of being part of her.

But first, let's talk about the triune nature of God. God has always existed as one God in three persons, also known as the Trinity. While the triune nature of God is one of the most challenging doctrines to understand, we can at least grasp the relational nature of God. We need to at least get our arms around this aspect of God's triune nature because it explains why God created—and why He didn't.

As one God in three persons, God has always enjoyed perfect relationship within His triune nature. God the Father, God the Son, and God the Spirit have always existed within a relationship of perfect unity and harmony. C. S. Lewis described this relationship as a dance.[19] A great, beautiful dance with the three moving as one. This is really a helpful way to think of it. Imagine the Father, the Son, and the Spirit moving together in perfect time with one another. This divine dance completely satisfies God. God did not create, as some wrongly suggest, because He was lonely and needed people He could relate to. God is fully satisfied in Himself! God did not create to get. God created to give.

When God created humankind, He invited them to partake in this beautiful dance. He created with the intention of allowing His love to overflow onto His creation for His glory. And the dance was even more amazing on a smaller scale as God designed Adam and Eve to be relational creatures, enjoying their own dance as husband and wife within the greater dance of God.

> God is fully satisfied in Himself! God did not create to get. God created to give.

Unfortunately, Adam and Eve (and all of humanity who would come after them) rebelled and were removed from the dance. But God is a pursuing God. Through Jesus, He provided a way for us to return to the dance. That is at the heart of the gospel: relationship restored in Christ.

And here is where the church comes in. Relationships are at the core of God's identity and heart. Just as God

---

19. C. S. Lewis, *Mere Christianity* (San Francisco, CA: HarperOne, 2015), 136.

created Adam and Eve to have relationship with Him and with each other, He has also designed us to be in relationship with Him and the church. Being part of a gospel community is not an option as some see it. It is a necessary expression of belief in the gospel. The gospel brings us into relationship with God and with the community of faith. This is most intimately experienced within the local church.

The local church does not merely present a way to gather and worship on a regular basis. Instead, the church offers us a group of people who will walk alongside us as we experience God's transforming power through the gospel. We encourage one another

> **Relationships are at the core of God's identity and heart.**

through the church. We lean into one another's lives, help each other fight sin, and practice accountability together. We share our struggles and our victories as the Spirit changes us—all while showing the world the beauty of community as God designed it to be.

We need the church. The world needs the church. This is why the dropout rate of church is so serious and why we must do whatever it takes to turn it around. Rather than teach behavior modification, we have to show kids the beauty of the gospel and help them understand the long-term process of gospel transformation.

Questions for Reflection and Discussion

- How are you beginning to lay foundations of faith in the hearts of preschoolers?
- If behavior change starts with the heart, how do we shepherd kids who have not yet trusted in Jesus?
- How do you provide positive guidance and discipline in the classroom for kids whose hearts are not being transformed?
- How do we measure spiritual maturity in our kids? How should we?
- How do we practice community in our kids ministry? Do we protect relationship-building time each week?
- How do we lovingly correct behavior while loving unconditionally?

Application: Gospel-Centered Transformation

1. **Develop a discipleship pathway for kids.** Consider the main periods and events during a child's spiritual growth and what they need to understand and experience during each one. Use this as a guide to help frame your evangelism and discipleship efforts.

- *Before trusting in Christ:* What is the gospel; obeying God because it is right and best for you
- *Trusting in Christ:* Why follow Jesus (not just to avoid hell); what it means to follow Jesus for life

- *Baptism and the Lord's Supper:* What they are; why we celebrate each; how they each are celebrated
- *After trusting in Christ:* Our continuing need of the gospel; living under grace; how sin impacts us as believers; living with urgency and hope in Christ's return; being part of the church

2. **Consider how to encourage and incorporate the spiritual disciplines in your ministry.**

- *Bible Reading:* Regular personal Bible reading
- *Journaling:* Drawing and/or writing reflections on Bible reading and your relationship with God
- *Prayer:* Regular personal times of prayer
- *Fasting:* Fasting food, non-food items (such as tech), or partial foods (such as sweets) for a period of time to focus more on God
- *Community:* Being part of meaningful community with other believing kids and families
- *Worship:* Regular times of worship both with the church and on their own
- *Serving:* Using gifts, resources, and abilities to advance the gospel
- *Stewardship:* Giving regularly, generously, sacrificially, and joyfully to the church and kingdom work
- *Evangelism:* Building friendships with unbelievers and sharing the gospel with others

3. **Calendar community-building activities and events.** Evaluate how many events and activities are scheduled with the major win of connecting kids with one another and families in your ministry together. Determine the right frequency of these activities and events and ensure they are calendared.

–PART 4–
GOSPEL-CENTERED MISSION

CHAPTER 20

LET'S GO: FINDING PURPOSE IN THE GOSPEL

The two travelers on the Emmaus Road experienced Jesus in a new and powerful way. They had known Old Testament stories and prophecies that morning, but by evening they understood them. Jesus had shown the two travelers how all the stories in the Old Testament fit together to tell one big story pointing to Him. After explaining the gospel narrative, Jesus then disappeared from their midst mid-meal.

Encountering the gospel changed the Emmaus disciples. The gospel has a funny way of doing that. When we truly encounter the gospel and are truly changed by it, we can't sit still. We have to do something, just like the two disciples did that evening.

That very hour they got up and returned to Jerusalem. They found the Eleven and those with them gathered together, who said, "The Lord has truly been raised and has appeared to Simon!" Then they began to describe what had happened on the road and how he was made known to them in the breaking of the bread. (Luke 24:33–35)

By the time the two disciples got up from their meal to return the six miles to Jerusalem, it was already dark. Earlier, when the pair had invited Jesus to eat with them, they had told Him it was "almost evening, and now the day is almost over" (Luke 24:29). By this time, it was surely evening. One thing you didn't want to do was travel from one city to the next in the dark. Traveling in the dark was dangerous because that was when robbers came out.

It would have made sense for the two disciples to have said something like, "That was amazing! The other disciples really have to hear about this! Let's get up early and go back to Jerusalem first thing so we can tell them!" That would have been completely reasonable, right? However, this wasn't what they did at all. They immediately got up and went directly back to Jerusalem in the dark. This is where we have to ask, "Why did these disciples take such a risk to travel at night instead of waiting until the morning?"

> Why did these disciples take such a risk to travel at night instead of waiting until the morning?

Here's the answer: They couldn't wait because they couldn't sit still after what they had just experienced. They had encountered the risen Christ. They had heard Him share the gospel and it penetrated deep into their hearts. Now, they had to act. When we encounter the gospel, we have to act. We can't contain ourselves. The gospel always prompts action.

They had heard Him share the gospel and it penetrated deep into their hearts. Now, they had to act.

The gospel leads to heart change, which leads to action. This is what the two Emmaus disciples experienced that day, and it is what we want each kid in our ministries to experience as well.

CHAPTER 21

FOLDING CARD TABLES: ARE KIDS THE CHURCH OF TOMORROW?

"Kids are the church of tomorrow." I cringe every time I hear this statement. Oh, I know most people don't mean any harm by it. They're simply trying to remind us that we need to raise the next generation to become future leaders in the church. However, it still pains me to hear this expression used.

That statement subtly implies that kids are not a vital part of the church today. It's as if our kids are sitting at the folding card table at Thanksgiving, waiting for the day when they can join the adults at the real table. This notion is about as far away from the truth as we can get. Theologically, functionally, and missionally, kids are an essential part of the church today. Right now.

The Theological Nature of Kids Being an Essential Part of the Church

Paul talked about the nature of the church quite a bit in his Epistles. The human body was one of his favorite metaphors to use. Paul talked about the church as a human body in Romans, 1 Corinthians, Colossians, and Ephesians. Here's one of his uses of bodily imagery:

There is one body and one Spirit—just as you were called to one hope at your calling—one Lord, one faith, one baptism, one God and Father of all, who is above all and through all and in all. (Eph. 4:4–6)

What word jumps out at you? What word does Paul use multiple times in that one sentence? That's right—*one*. One body. One Spirit. One hope. One Lord. One faith. One baptism. One God.

The word *one* is used seven times out of the 40 total words in that sentence. That's almost a fifth of the passage dedicated to one word! Most writers go out of their way to use synonyms instead of repeating the same word. So why did Paul use the word *one* so many times? It was because he was making an important point, one he wanted to be abundantly clear about.

Just as a person has one body, not two or three, there is one church. There isn't a past church, a present church, and a future church. There isn't a JV team church or a minor league church. There is simply *the* church. One church. Kids who have trusted in Christ are part of that one church.

When a kid trusts in Christ, everything that is true about salvation is true of her in that instant. She is a new creation. The old is gone and the new has come. She is completely forgiven, completely righteous, completely justified. She has become a child of God with full access to her Father through the Son by the power of the Spirit. She has been brought into God's family fully and completely—to share in relationship and accountability and to play her unique role in the mission of the church.

What is true of you in Christ? That is also exactly true of the eight-year-old who trusted in Christ last week! And that's why we cannot say kids are the church of tomorrow. It reduces these saints to second-class citizens in Christ's kingdom. They have a role to play in God's kingdom right now as they answer to their King.

The Functional Nature of Kids Being an Essential Part of the Church

The beauty of Paul's metaphor of the church as a human body is that it allows for striking diversity within uncompromising unity. A human body has many different parts, each with different functions, that all work together in harmony. In the same way, God's design is for the church to be one unified body, but for that body to be made

> **Just as a person has one body, not two or three, there is one church. . . . Kids who have trusted in Christ are part of that one church.**

up of very different people, each fulfilling his or her unique role to accomplish the church's one mission.

When a church looks and acts like this, it is a sight to behold. It's beautiful when people who are very different unite in Christ. A church full of people who genuinely love one another and embrace their differences makes for a powerful picture of the gospel. The church shouldn't turn a blind eye to these differences. She should celebrate them because God has brought such beautifully different people together as one in Christ.[20] God is certainly glorified in a diverse, unified church.

> **God is certainly glorified in a diverse, unified church.**

A unified church full of diverse people is also quite functional. Let's go back to Paul's body metaphor, this time in Romans, to see how this is true:

> **Now as we have many parts in one body, and all the parts do not have the same function, in the same way we who are many are one body in Christ and individually members of one another. (Rom. 12:4–5)**

Imagine if the human body were made up of only eyes. While we might be able to see well (and actually, we couldn't do that without a brain), we wouldn't be able to hear, taste,

---

20. Revelation 7:9.

touch, move, breathe, or do anything else. This wouldn't be a good design for a body, would it?

In the same way, God didn't design the church body to be full of people who are the same. He gives us diversity of ideas, experiences, talents, skills, and giftings so that together we can function at full capacity.

Our kids who have trusted in Christ are part of that wonderful design. God has given each child ideas, experiences, talents, skills, and giftings to be used for the church's mission to bring God glory. Just as the human body would not function at full capacity if you removed parts of it—such as the hands—we cannot expect the church body to operate at full capacity if we remove parts of it—such as our kids!

One of the things I love about kids is their energy and joy. Yes, that energy can be hard to bear at times, especially when it's time to talk about a Bible story and they'd rather throw index cards at a cabinet to see who can get a card to stick in the gap between the door and the cabinet (true story). However, that energy and joy is actually a gift to the church. It's hard to spend time with kids and not be energized. It's hard to talk with kids for long and not laugh and smile. It would be our loss if kids were pushed to the margins of the church.

However, there is an even more profound gift that kids provide the church:

He [Jesus] called a child and had him stand among them. "Truly I tell you," he said, "unless you turn and become like children, you will never enter the kingdom of heaven. Therefore, whoever humbles himself like this child—this one is the

greatest in the kingdom of heaven. And whoever welcomes one child like this in my name welcomes me." (Matt. 18:2–5)

We often hear the take-away of this passage taught as though we should strive for childlike faith. That isn't quite what Jesus was talking about. Instead, Jesus used a child to teach about a person's need to have childlike *humility*—a humility that will in turn lead to saving faith.

My youngest son Caleb loves drinking smoothies that come vacuum-sealed with foil. He drinks several of these a day and each time brings them to my wife or me to open. He has no qualms about this. He knows he cannot pull that piece of foil hard enough to open the smoothie, but it doesn't embarrass him. He doesn't make excuses for why he cannot open it. He just shamelessly brings the smoothie to us to open.

> Childlike humility leads to this kind of saving faith. This beautiful model of humility is another gift that kids provide the church.

This is a simple picture of the humility Jesus was talking about. Kids know they need help. They know there is so much they cannot do. And this truth doesn't shame them. They accept it and get help.

That kind of humility—that forces you to depend on someone else—is at the core of the gospel. To properly receive the gospel we need to admit that we cannot do anything about our sin on our own. We need help. We need to fully depend on Jesus to take care of the problem of sin for us. Childlike humility leads to this kind of saving faith. This beautiful model of humility is another gift that kids provide the church.

Every time we see kids shamelessly asking for someone to help them find a Bible verse, asking who made God, or if their pet will be in heaven—we should cherish their humility as a gift to the church and ask ourselves if we are walking in this kind of humility.

The Missional Nature of Kids Being an Essential Part of the Church

Kids who have trusted in Jesus have so much to offer the church as she gathers. However, kids also have much to offer the church as she is scattered throughout the week on mission. This is a mission that centers on evangelism.

I thought of something a few years ago that has really stuck with me. You may have thought of it too; I am sure the thought isn't original to me. Almost everything we do now for God, we will do better in eternity when sin is finally removed from our lives. We will learn better. We will love better. We will serve better. We will worship better. Almost everything we do for God's glory will be done better in eternity.

But there is one thing we won't do better. In fact, we won't be able to do it at all—share the gospel. Evangelism is one of the few things we can only do now. This makes evangelism central to our mission. (Well, that and the fact that Jesus commanded us to share the gospel.) If evangelism is central to the church's mission, and if kids are indeed an important part of the church, then we should actively be encouraging kids to evangelize.

As we tell our kids the one big story of Jesus, we need to be sure they understand that His story is still ongoing and that they have a role to play in it. God has placed our kids where they are to bring about a revolution through the gospel. This is the vision we must cast to them.

God has placed our kids where they are to bring about a revolution through the gospel. This is the vision we must cast to them.

CHAPTER 22

ONE CHURCH, ONE MISSION

Jesus summed up the church's mission at the end of the book of Matthew in a passage we know as the Great Commission. While that passage may be familiar to many, it's worth noting that the other three Gospels end, and the book of Acts begins, with similar commissions. This is how important it is for the church to understand her mission and that her mission includes kids.

> **Jesus came near and said to them, "All authority has been given to me in heaven and on earth. Go, therefore, and make disciples of all nations, baptizing them in the name of the Father and of the Son and of the Holy Spirit, teaching them to observe everything I have commanded you. And**

remember, I am with you always, to the end of the age." (Matt. 28:18–20)

Jesus begins this passage by stating the authority He has as Head of the church. Indeed, all authority is His. Starting the commission off with this reminder serves two purposes. First, it makes what follows a command, not a suggestion. Second, it reminds us that the success of the mission ultimately depends on Jesus, not on us. Jesus not only has authority over His church, but He also has authority over the entire world—including those who would oppose the bride of Christ.

In this authority, Jesus commands the church to go. We must never forget that we are a sent church, not an entrenched church. The latter has been the posture of far too many churches for far too long. "We're going to stay right here. You know where we are. You're welcome to visit anytime you like. Just be sure to dress and act right if you do come."

This sentiment is not what Christ commanded, nor is it what He modeled. Jesus didn't command His church to do anything He wasn't willing to do Himself. Jesus left His place in glory, humbled Himself, and came to Earth in human flesh. Even His earthly ministry was modeled around the word *go* as He traveled from town to town. Christ didn't set up shop in Nazareth and wait for people to come to Him. No, Jesus truly showed us what "go" looks like.

That little two-letter word *go* is even richer when we understand it carries with it the idea of an ongoing process. You can think of it as, "As you are going. . . ." Going should not be done at certain times or in certain seasons. Going should happen daily, as a normal rhythm of life.

Understanding "go" this way is critical because we cannot fulfill the Great Commission in only structured, programmed contexts. There's nothing wrong with programmed evangelism opportunities—unless that is the only way we're trying to fulfill the Great Commission. If we want to obey Jesus' command and complete the mission He gave us, then we have to make living on mission a part of our daily lives.

> **Going should not be done at certain times or in certain seasons. Going should happen daily, as a normal rhythm of life.**

We are to be on mission wherever we are, doing whatever we're doing. It's not just a ministry program on Tuesday nights at 6:00 p.m. It's a way of life.

And what does Jesus want us to do as a normal rhythm of our lives? We are to make disciples. A disciple is a follower of Jesus. A person—man, woman, or child—who has trusted in Jesus in response to the gospel, has been given new life in Christ, and has begun the process of gospel transformation. Of course, evangelism is a critical part of making disciples, but look at the two accompanying participles that add flavor to our task. We are to make disciples. That includes baptizing and teaching.

Baptizing reminds us of the need to bring these new disciples into gospel community. We most often think of baptism as a picture of a new believer being united with

Christ,[21] but it is also a picture of that believer being united with the bride of Christ, the Church.[22] The New Testament is clear that God's will is for every believer to be connected to a local church.

Teaching reminds us of the need to help others experience gospel transformation and to live joyfully in a way that pleases God.[23] Part of this teaching is to share the mission of the church in which new disciples become disciple-makers who in turn continue to make other new disciples. This is a process that will continue until Christ returns.[24]

Jesus concluded the Great Commission by reminding us that He will be with us always—a great comfort. We are not on this mission alone and, again, it will not be completed in our power, but His.

> We are not on this mission alone and, again, it will not be completed in our power, but His.

---

21. Romans 6:3–6.
22. 1 Corinthians 12:13.
23. Ephesians 4:11–16.
24. 2 Timothy 2:2.

CHAPTER 23

KIDS ON MISSION

OK. I know what you might be thinking.

"I'm with you about teaching our kids the gospel and allowing the gospel to change them. I'm good with kids being part of the church today. And I can even get my arms around how kids are supposed to be on mission. But here's where I'm having some trouble. How are kids supposed to do this? How does an eight-year-old girl make disciples?"

Great question! I'm glad you asked it, because the answer is important. Here it is: Kids make disciples the same way we do, which is the same way Jesus did. Jesus gave us a great picture of what living out this mission looks like midway through His earthly ministry.

Jesus continued going around to all the towns and villages, teaching in their synagogues, preaching the good news of the kingdom, and

healing every disease and every sickness. When he saw the crowds, he felt compassion for them, because they were distressed and dejected, like sheep without a shepherd. Then he said to his disciples, "The harvest is abundant, but the workers are few. Therefore, pray to the Lord of the harvest to send out workers into his harvest." (Matt. 9:35–38)

Notice that, as usual, Jesus was on the move. However, Jesus wasn't selective about where He went—He went to all the towns and villages. That's an important lesson for us. Sometimes we struggle to go at all, and when we finally do go, we can be selective about where exactly we go. We go to the safe places. We go to the comfortable places. We go to places with people who are like us—they look like us, sound like us, and act like us. Or we go to the places that we think will bear the most fruit. Places where people are more likely to respond to the gospel. Jesus didn't do any of that. He went. He simply went—everywhere.

Let's also look at what Jesus did while He was on the go. He taught. He preached. He healed. In the "going" and "doing" Jesus demonstrates His heart for people. He felt compassion for the crowds because they were weary and worn out from trying to live the right way to please God. That didn't frustrate Jesus—He didn't sigh and give them grief for not getting it. Jesus was moved deeply by the people.

We see that Jesus met the spiritual needs (teaching and preaching), the physical needs (healing), and emotional needs (compassion) of the people. This is what our kids need to do as well.

Several years ago a movement developed that emphasized meeting the physical needs of people through missions. The movement went too far though, and some missionaries served for years without ever sharing the gospel. Meanwhile, there are Christians who will share the gospel but don't consider it important to do anything else to meet people's physical or emotional needs.

Both of these missional strategies are incomplete. Don't take my word for it; look at Jesus' example. Jesus didn't just heal sick people—He pointed them to salvation too. Jesus didn't just preach and teach; He healed people (even though every single person He physically healed eventually died). This didn't stop Him from healing though—because Jesus' love for people wouldn't let Him do that. Moreover, when Jesus healed people, He gave the Father glory and revealed the truth that He is the Savior.

While a case can be made that evangelism is paramount to mercy ministries, we cannot share the gospel in a vacuum divorced from caring about people's other needs. We should feed the hungry, clothe the poor, encourage the distressed, and fight against the injustices of the oppressed.[25] We should do all these things while we proclaim the beauty of the gospel. Kids are also called to share the gospel and meet people's needs. Here are some ideas for encouraging this lifestyle in your kids ministry:

Spiritual Needs: If we are teaching kids the big story of the Bible (the gospel) and helping them understand gospel transformation rather than behavior modification, then we're also giving them a solid understanding of how to

---

25. James 2:15–17; Amos 5:21–24; Matthew 25:31–46.

share the gospel with others. If a kid has trusted in Jesus, she understands the message of salvation and can simply share what she knows with others. However, we don't want our kids to have to figure this out on their own. Instead, we can help equip them as missionaries by reminding them that they know the gospel well enough to share it. We also foster evangelistic confidence in kids by helping them talk through the basics of the gospel. An excellent tool to help train kids in this area is *The Gospel: God's Plan for Me.*[26]

I want to encourage you to ask your kids about friends they may have who don't know Jesus. Guide your group to pray for their friends and regularly ask if anyone has shared the gospel with a friend recently.

Physical Needs: It's probably easier for most of us to think of ways our kids can be part of meeting physical needs than the other two types of needs. Collecting coats, clothes, food, school supplies, and other items is a great way for kids to help meet physical needs. Serving at soup kitchens and shelters is another great opportunity.

> If we are teaching kids the big story of the Bible (the gospel) and helping them understand gospel transformation rather than behavior modification, then we're also giving them a solid understanding of how to share the gospel with others.

---

26. Available from lifeway.com.

As you think of ways to encourage your kids in this area, be careful not to exclude ways kids can meet physical needs on their own—as part of their normal rhythm of life. Perhaps a kid can "adopt" an elderly neighbor and help mow the lawn, weed the flower beds, rake leaves, and shovel snow for them on a regular basis. Kids can also be encouraged to sell some of their possessions at a yard sale or use chore money to help families they know who are in need.

Emotional Needs: Of the three types of needs, this is the one that is perhaps most often overlooked and may be the hardest for kids. It's also hard for many adults! But that doesn't mean kids can't meet the emotional needs of others. A great way to begin developing this attitude in kids is to regularly talk about local, national, and international missions. Cast a vision that many people are hurting around the world and that God desires to use His church to comfort them.

If you're a teacher, a kids worship leader, or if you serve in some other role involving a group of kids, you can also teach your kids to meet emotional needs through the way you lead. Kids are selfish by nature. (Actually, so are adults!) Kids have trouble thinking of others before themselves, which is why they will interrupt one another without much thought and want to be the first one to get a snack. Use these opportunities to teach about selflessness and empathy. Help your kids truly feel for others.

As Jesus was meeting the spiritual, physical, and emotional needs of the people around Him, He looked at the number of people around Him and told the disciples that the harvest was abundant and ripe. However, they needed to pray for more workers. There was so much need.[27] If you continue reading into the next chapter, you'll see that Jesus sends the twelve disciples out on mission after this.[28] They were the answer to their own prayer! They were the workers Jesus was looking for. Jesus told them to pray for workers first because He wanted them to see that mission started with them. Harvesting the fields always starts with *me* before *they*.

The fields are just as ripe today. The Great Commission is no less urgent. We need workers for the fields, and once again, it starts close by—with you and your kids ministry.

---

27. Matthew 9:37–38.
28. Matthew 10:5–15.

CHAPTER 24

A RIPE MISSION FIELD

Remember that the gospel transforms. When the gospel gets into a person's heart, it will naturally affect how they live. Part of this is joining in Jesus' story—a story that continues to unfold today through His church. That is what living on mission is all about—being part of Jesus' story in the context of your daily life.

This is also what Jesus invites our kids to be part of. Right now. Not just later when they get "old enough." A kid who has trusted in Jesus is a missionary. Period. Full stop. No qualifiers.

The tragedy in many churches today is that we fail to see our kids as missionaries. We're content to see them as buckets instead of pipes. Let me explain. A bucket is designed to collect something, let's say water. If you had a leaky faucet, you would put a bucket under it to collect the water. The bucket would hold the water and keep it from running onto the floor and causing damage. Buckets keep things contained.

A pipe on the other hand is designed to move things along. Again, think of the plumbing pipes in a house. They don't keep the water in one place—they channel it. Pipes move water to where you want it to be and release water for its intended purpose (drinking, bathing, washing, and so forth). Buckets keep. Pipes transfer.

When I say that many churches see their kids as buckets, I mean that they see their kids as collectors of something—of Bible knowledge or perhaps even the gospel. The vision of these churches is to fill each bucket up as much as possible. This would sound great if discipleship were all about us. However, we know it's not. Discipleship is about making disciple-makers. This is why we have to see our kids as pipes.

We need to pour the gospel into our kids, not with the aim of only filling them up, but with the goal of moving the gospel through them. They accomplish this by sharing the gospel and by putting it to work wherever they go. This is where it gets exciting. Really exciting.

Most people who trust in Jesus will do so before they turn eighteen. If you were to talk to ten Christians, about four of them would have trusted in Jesus before they turned thirteen. Two more would have become Christians before they turned eighteen, and one more would have responded to the gospel before turning twenty-one.[29] Statistically, the ripest harvest field for the gospel falls in the demographic of kids. Other than their parents, who is better at reaching

---

29. "Evangelism Is Most Effective Among Kids," Research Releases in Family & Kids, 11 October 2004 [6 February 2017]. Available on the Internet: https://www.barna.com/research.

kids than kids themselves? Kids have access to kids. Kids naturally relate to each other.

Our failure to cast a vision of our kids as missionaries (a vision by which we equip, empower, and encourage them) has left this ripe mission field short of workers. If we're praying for the gospel to take route in the next generation, we must mobilize this untapped missionary force in our churches. Can you imagine how many more kids would trust in Jesus if they heard the gospel from our kids? Can you also imagine what would then happen in these kids' families and in your city after that? You want to see the Great Commission fulfilled in your city? Start by seeing your kids as missionaries.

So where can your kids be on mission in your city? Well, where do they spend their time? School. Sports teams. Dance squads. Clubs. Neighborhoods. Homes. Summer camps. This is their mission field.

We need to help our kids see that God has placed them exactly where they are for a purpose. Our kids need to know they can perform any activity for God's glory as they play their role in Jesus' ongoing story. Our kids also need to see the unique potential they have to impact their friends with the gospel as they seek to live as pipes, not as buckets.

Imagine if your ministry was filled with kids who helped to meet the physical, emotional, and spiritual needs of other kids. Imagine if those kids served as disciple-making disciples who were being changed by the gospel day-by-day. Imagine kids growing together in community with other kids because everyone is on mission together. That's exciting kids ministry. That's gospel-centered kids ministry!

Questions for Reflection and Discussion

- Are you teaching all kids, even preschoolers, to be missional as Jesus was?
- Is your kids ministry's missions strategy integrated with the vision and strategy of the entire church? Why or why not?
- Do you cast a big vision for your kids of what it means to be on mission? How can you expand that vision?
- Are you modeling and teaching generosity?
- What are some practical ways you can encourage and equip preschool and elementary kids to meet the spiritual needs around them? What about physical and emotional needs?
- Is your ministry equipping parents to lead their kids to be on mission as a family?

Application: Gospel-Centered Mission

1. **Develop and conduct evangelism coaching.** Just as many adults need help to learn how to share their faith with others, your kids may too. Develop a seminar or class to ensure your kids understand the basics of the gospel and learn some ways to talk with others about the gospel. Consider using "The Gospel: God's Plan for Us:"

- *God Rules*
- *We Sinned*
- *God Provided*

- *Jesus Gives*
- *We Respond*

2. **Develop and implement an organized missions focus.** While we want to encourage our kids to live on mission in their normal rhythms of life, we also need to include organized missions opportunities through our ministries. Consider the following factors:

- *Local, regional, national, and international partnerships and opportunities:* It's important to show that we are to be concerned with spreading the gospel where we live and to the ends of the world.
- *Family involvement:* Part of missions is certainly praying for missionaries, giving funds to support missionaries, and collecting resources to send to missionaries for their use, but it is more than that. We want to help engage our children, and their families, to be on mission.
- *Special events:* Consider special days and times throughout the year that provide natural emphases for missions, such as Easter, Christmas, the Olympic Games, etc.

3. **Incorporate missions visuals in your ministry space.** The old adage of "out of sight, out of mind" can certainly hold true. Walk around your kids ministry space and consider how you can incorporate missions visuals such as maps, information about people groups, information about missionaries you support, etc.

–PART 5–

GOSPEL-
CENTERED
LEADERS

CHAPTER 25

LEAD THE WAY: THE WEIGHTINESS OF LEADERSHIP

Saul was a man clearly marked by the gospel. Before his conversion, he had been the prototypical Pharisee.[30] Circumcised on the eighth day. Of the tribe of Benjamin. A Hebrew. A Pharisee. Defender of the Jewish faith by persecuting the church. Strict adherent of the law.

From all appearances, Saul seemed like a perfect Jew. Yet he was dead on the inside. He was a whitewashed tomb. Then one day Saul met Jesus—or to be more precise, Jesus met him. As Saul walked along the Damascus Road, Jesus appeared to him in a light that was so bright it blinded the Pharisee. Ironically, though his physical sight was hindered,

---

30. Philippians 3:5–6.

Saul was able to see spiritual truth for the first time as he came to know the living Christ.

God used Saul's conversion to dramatically change the world around him. In fact, the reverberations of Saul's conversion can still be felt throughout the church today. After going away for some time to learn the gospel and prepare for a life of ministry, Saul—who was also known as Paul—began his relentless pursuit of sharing the gospel wherever he could, no matter what it cost him. Over the next three decades, God used Paul to plant churches throughout the Roman Empire and to write letters, under the inspiration of the Holy Spirit, that continue to be the catalyst to plant churches around the world today.

When Paul encountered the gospel, it transformed him so that he couldn't sit still. He invested the rest of his life, despite enduring multiple hardships, to join in Jesus' ongoing story. By the time Paul breathed his last, God had used him as an extremely effective missionary, church planter, and as one of the most influential theologians of all time.

As a missionary and church planter, Paul saw the need to expand the church to the outermost parts of the Roman Empire—including Rome itself. As a theologian, Paul knew that the early church had to be built on a solid, gospel-centered foundation to stand the test of time. He knew that Israel had wavered in her faithfulness to God throughout her history. As a former Pharisee whose obedience was motivated by pride, not a love for God, Paul knew first-hand just how dangerous moralism could be.

Paul recognized that the long-term health and vitality of the churches God planted through him largely depended on their leaders. If the churches were shepherded by gospel-centered leaders, they would be in good shape. However, if the churches were led by people with priorities other than the gospel, the churches would crumble. It was critical to grow leaders who would love God, desire to live out the gospel, and help their churches do the same.

Three of Paul's letters—1 Timothy, 2 Timothy, and Titus—were written with this aim in mind. In each of these letters, collectively known as the Pastoral Epistles, Paul wrote to younger pastors to encourage them. He reminded them of their calling to pastor in the power of the gospel and for the sake of the gospel. He implored them to appoint godly leaders to serve alongside them in this work. Paul's heart and concern for godly leadership is not merely confined to these three letters. We find it elsewhere in his writings, such as in this passage in Ephesians:

> **And he himself gave some to be apostles, some evangelists, some pastors and teachers, equipping the saints for the work of ministry, to build up the body of Christ, until we all reach unity in the faith and in the knowledge of God's Son, growing into maturity with a stature measured by Christ's fullness. Then we will no longer be little children, tossed by the waves and blown around by every wind of teaching, by human cunning with cleverness in the techniques of deceit. But speaking the truth in love, let us grow in every way into him who is the head—Christ. From him the whole body, fitted and knit together by every supporting ligament, promotes the growth of the**

**body for building up itself in love by the proper
working of each individual part. (Eph. 4:11–16)**

Godly church leaders are important because they equip the saints to grow in maturity through the gospel. We're all experiencing gospel transformation (perhaps to different degrees or at different paces), but one trait we should all have in common is that we're moving in the same direction—toward Christlikeness. This also includes leaders. However, leaders aren't only responsible for their own spiritual maturity; they also play an important role in coming alongside other believers and encouraging them, equipping them, empowering them, pushing them, pulling them, and sometimes, even dragging them toward the fullness of the gospel.

> To be a leader is to accept a weighty calling.

To be a leader is to accept a weighty calling. It isn't easy nor is it glamorous. It isn't rewarding from an earthly perspective. However, it's a noble calling that bears fruit for eternity.

CHAPTER 26

WE NEED YOU: RECRUITING WITH HONESTY

People don't usually line up to serve in kids ministry. Yet, there always seem to be volunteer holes that need to be filled right away. We plead, beg, bargain, cajole, and sometimes even guilt people into service. We'll do whatever it takes to fill the vacant spots in our kids ministry for one more week. Indeed, our kids ministry volunteer application may consist of just three questions:

1. Do you love Jesus?
2. Can you pass a background check?
3. Are you alive?

A footnote on the application might even indicate that sometimes we'll accept just two Yes answers. Sometimes just one.

I know this sounds harsh. However, we need to come to terms with where many of our ministries are regarding staffing. If we don't acknowledge this reality, we cannot begin to fix it. And we must fix it fast! As long as this problem exists, the gospel-centeredness of our ministries will be hindered.

You see, as long as we recruit with a beggar's posture, we will never develop the kind of leaders we need in kids ministry—leaders who are living out Ephesians 4. We need leaders who help kids see the gospel, love the gospel, grow in the gospel, and dedicate their lives to the gospel. Leaders who are just filling volunteer holes don't do that. We need gospel-centered and gospel-motivated leaders who are willing to do whatever it takes. Leaders for whom failure is not an option. You want a recruiting slogan for your ministry? Try this one:

Not many should become teachers, my brothers, because you know that we will receive a stricter judgment. (James 3:1)

Seems backward, doesn't it? This is the very last thing we would want to tell a prospective kids leader. "Hey, come teach in kids ministry and be held to a stricter judgment by God! OK, great! So do you want to serve during the first service or the second? Do you prefer kids who are not potty trained or who are able to read and write? By the way, what's your T-shirt size?"

But that is exactly what prospective leaders need to hear and what we need to get into their hearts. You see, at the core of James's warning is this reality: teaching is important. We shouldn't take teaching lightly because God certainly doesn't.

Jesus used a similar recruiting slogan when He saw large crowds following Him:

> **Now great crowds were traveling with him. So he turned and said to them: "If anyone comes to me and does not hate his own father and mother, wife and children, brothers and sisters—yes, and even his own life—he cannot be my disciple. Whoever does not bear his own cross and come after me cannot be my disciple." (Luke 14:25–27)**

Once again, this seems counterintuitive. Didn't Jesus come to Earth to draw people to Himself? Wasn't this huge crowd a win for Him? Yet, instead of celebrating or encouraging the crowd to invite others to follow Him, Jesus seemed to want to chase them off. You have to hate your family to follow Him? You have to carry a cross? What's going on here? Before we can answer this, let's first make sure we understand what Jesus meant by hating your family and carrying a cross.

It's jarring to hear Jesus say we have to hate our families to follow Him. It just feels completely wrong. Aren't we supposed to love others? An important rule of thumb for Bible study is to always interpret what is unclear in light of what is clear. Loving others and honoring our parents are clear teachings in Scripture. So we start with that. Jesus cannot mean we must literally hate our families because that would contradict the clear teaching of Scripture.

There are two prevailing explanations of what Jesus meant by saying we must hate our families. The first, and perhaps most common one, is that Jesus was offering a stark point of contrast between our love for Him and our love for our families. If we want to follow Jesus, we need to love Him with such a profound love that the deep love for our families pales in comparison and actually seems like hate.

Teaching is important. We shouldn't take teaching lightly because God certainly doesn't.

Another explanation is that Jesus was using a cultural idiom for choosing one thing over another. You choose, or love, one thing and reject, or hate, the other. We see an example of this in Romans 9:13 where Paul says God loved Jacob and hated Esau meaning that God chose Jacob over Esau to be the son of promise and continue the line of Christ.

I believe this second explanation is what Jesus meant. A person who wants to follow Jesus—truly follow Him unlike the superficial crowds who were following Him for what He could do for them—has to choose Jesus above everything else, even family and his own life. That fits with what Jesus then said about carrying a cross.

We see the cross quite differently today than how Jesus' original audience understood it. For us, the cross is a sign of hope and triumph. We associate the cross with victory and often wear it as jewelry. However, the crowd gathered around

Jesus that day saw the cross quite differently. For them, the cross meant one thing: death. This was not just any death; it was a terribly painful and shameful death. We have to understand what Jesus meant in light of how the crowd that day would have understood His imagery. Jesus was telling the crowd in no uncertain terms that if they wanted to follow Him, they had to die for Him. Literally, as some would, and figuratively, as all should.

When Jesus looked out at the large crowd that day, He knew they were following Him for the wrong reasons and that they weren't truly committed. Jesus didn't want superficial followers. He wanted people who fully understood what it meant to follow Him and who were willing to do whatever it takes. This is why Jesus followed up these statements

> Someone who isn't willing to go all in as Jesus' disciple should not attempt to follow Him. Following Jesus half-heartedly doesn't work. The cost is too great and the mission is too important.

with two stories that illustrated counting the cost of discipleship.

A builder shouldn't begin construction on a tower if he doesn't have money to complete the project. Likewise, a king shouldn't engage in battle if he doesn't have the right-sized army to win.[31] In the same manner, someone who isn't

---

31. Luke 14:28–33.

willing to go all in as Jesus' disciple should not attempt to follow Him. Following Jesus half-heartedly doesn't work. The cost is too great and the mission is too important.

That is why we want our recruitment efforts to communicate the weightiness of the mission of kids ministry. Kids leaders are too important. If we don't expect much, we won't get much. A lowered bar may let more people in, but it also becomes a tripping hazard.

Instead of inviting people to fill a hole or keep kids alive and perhaps teach a little bit of the Bible for an hour or so, we need to cast the vision that we are offering them the opportunity to do something enormous for God. They can be part of one of the most important ministries in the church—teaching kids the gospel!

CHAPTER 27

GOSPEL TEACHING: THE KIDS LEADER AS A THEOLOGIAN

Every kids leader is a theologian. I can say that because everyone is a theologian. The only question is whether we are good ones or bad ones.

When most of us think of theologians, we perhaps think of professors wearing suede sport coats with elbow patches, debating obscure intricacies of the faith such as whether Jesus ever got a cold or if Adam had a belly button. But theology is simply a person's understanding of God. Under this definition, everyone's a theologian because everyone has some understanding of God. Again, the question is whether or not we have a proper understanding of God. This is what makes us good theologians or bad ones.

As kids leaders, it's critical that we have a correct understanding of God, because our kids are developing their own understanding of God based (at least in part) on what they hear from us. Let that sink in. This is precisely why James warned us not to desire to become teachers too quickly. That is one of the burdens we bear as kids leaders.

Kids leaders might not be thought of as theologians by many people, but I believe we should be some of the most sound theologians in the church. We play such an important role in establishing theological foundations in our kids, and those foundations have to be made out of rock, not sand. If our theology is weak as leaders, we are virtually dooming our kids to have a shaky theology as well.

That is why we need to embrace our role as theologians. We need to shatter the notion that kids leaders aren't theologians or that we just have to know the basics of our faith. Sure, we need to know the basics and be able to teach the basics to our kids, but we also need to be developing our theology and deepening our understanding of the gospel so that we can teach with greater clarity and conviction. We also need to be prepared to help our kids as they grow in their understanding of the gospel and wrestle with deeper issues. In times like this, our kids need us to be theologians.

We can learn quite a bit about not settling and growing as theologians from a man named Apollos. We encounter Apollos midway through the book of Acts:

> **Now a Jew named Apollos, a native Alexandrian, an eloquent man who was competent in the use of the Scriptures, arrived in Ephesus. He had been instructed in the way of the Lord; and being**

fervent in spirit, he was speaking and teaching accurately about Jesus, although he knew only John's baptism. He began to speak boldly in the synagogue. After Priscilla and Aquila heard him, they took him aside and explained the way of God to him more accurately. When he wanted to cross over to Achaia, the brothers and sisters wrote to the disciples to welcome him. After he arrived, he was a great help to those who by grace had believed. For he vigorously refuted the Jews in public, demonstrating through the Scriptures that Jesus is the Messiah. (Acts 18:24–28)

Look at what Apollos had going for him. He was eloquent. He could teach the Bible powerfully. He was passionate. Apollos would be the star kids volunteer in most churches today. Yet when Aquila and Priscilla heard him teach, they realized he had a hole in his theology, so they pulled him aside and taught him a more accurate theology. I love that! Aquila and Priscilla weren't satisfied with a powerful teacher who had his theology "mostly right." They wanted to help Apollos become a better teacher by refining his theology. By God's grace, he listened.

This needs to be our attitude as kids leaders. If we want to be good teachers, we have to be good learners. We can never be satisfied with where we are in our understanding of the gospel. Like Apollos, we need to be willing to stretch ourselves and learn the gospel more accurately. Teaching the gospel to kids can be challenging. At times, we will have to interact with weighty subjects like sin and death. We will have to be able to explain how Jesus dying on a cross two thousand years ago makes a difference for us today. We will have to be able to share how God sees us in Christ and what impact sin has on us as believers. Those are some theological issues that many kids leaders don't dive into, but we have to. We can't teach what we don't know ourselves.

Does this take time and effort on our part? Absolutely! But remember, teaching kids is a weighty responsibility with enormous potential kingdom impact. Our kids are worth the extra effort. Christ is worth the extra effort.

Thankfully, there are a number of resources to help you grow in the gospel and to help you customize what you are teaching for your kids and your context. Many kids curriculum come with materials for leaders, such as leader Bible studies, blog posts, and even training videos. Put these tools, resources from your church, and other blogs and podcasts to good use.

You may also want to build a personal library to include theology books, kids ministry books, and reference books such as commentaries and Bible dictionaries. Again, this might mean that you need to protect more time to read, study, and talk about the gospel with others.

Remember, our best teaching will always come from the overflow of our hearts and minds. The better theologians we are and the more captivated we are by the beauty of the gospel, the more we will have to give our kids. You are a theologian! Be a good one.

CHAPTER 28

GOSPEL TRANSFORMATION: THE KIDS LEADER AS A DISCIPLE

When churches look for a pastor, what do they most often look for? In many cases, it's how well a pastor preaches and teaches, how good he is at evangelism, and perhaps how strong of a leader he is. In other words, they look for skills. Is he skilled in an area that the church prioritizes or needs?

But look at what God focuses on in a pastor, or overseer:

> **An overseer, therefore, must be above reproach, the husband of one wife, self-controlled, sensible, respectable, hospitable, able to teach, not an excessive drinker, not a bully but gentle, not**

quarrelsome, not greedy. He must manage his own household competently and have his children under control with all dignity. (If anyone does not know how to manage his own household, how will he take care of God's church?) He must not be a new convert, or he might become conceited and incur the same condemnation as the devil. Furthermore, he must have a good reputation among outsiders, so that he does not fall into disgrace and the devil's trap. (1 Tim. 3:2–7)

God cares about character more than He cares about competence. Think about it. God has more to say about how a pastor engages family members than how well he preaches.

You can learn to preach or teach better. You can learn to lead better. You can learn to organize programs better. But one thing that is hard to learn is character. Character comes from gospel transformation and it reveals how deeply the gospel has impacted someone. A gospel-saturated man who can't preach his way out of a bag can still develop into a great pastor. However, a man who can preach beautiful sermons but who hasn't been deeply moved by the gospel will struggle to lead in a way that produces real fruit for the kingdom. Our churches need more of the former and fewer of the latter. We need people who have been deeply moved by the gospel and who are willing to be grown and stretched in whatever role God has called them into—pastor, kids director, and kids volunteer alike.

In many ways, being a kids ministry leader is a lot like being a pastor. We love our kids and provide listening ears for them. We challenge our kids and encourage them to step out in faith for Christ. And, of course, we teach our kids the gospel.

While God cares more about character than competency, that doesn't mean that we shouldn't strive to be excellent in all we do. Listen to what Paul told Timothy about his gifts of teaching and pastoring:

> **Practice these things; be committed to them, so that your progress may be evident to all. (1 Tim. 4:15)**

Timothy was to practice. He was to develop and progress in his ministry skills. He was supposed to work. This takes us back to our earlier discussions of being a theologian. We are to work on these areas and grow. However, at the same time, we can never forget that what matters most to our kids is their ability to see daily gospel transformation as disciples. Our kids will remember what we do, what kind of person we are, and how much we love them much longer than they will remember what we tell them.

> While God cares more about character than competency, that doesn't mean that we shouldn't strive to be excellent in all we do.

This means we need to be appropriately transparent with our kids and be quick to share our struggles, questions, victories, and failures with them on their level of understanding.

Our kids don't need perfect know-it-alls. They know none of those exist! They also don't need teachers who tell about their marital struggles or dating challenges. That would be inappropriate. Instead, kids need leaders who care enough for them to be real with them and readily share the areas of their lives where they need God to continue to work. The best teaching you can provide your kids is gospel-centered teaching that is infused with personal stories of your growth in the gospel.

As we seek to be transparent with our kids, we model in appropriate ways what we want them to experience. We want our kids to live on mission at the ball field, at school, and in the neighborhoods in which they live. We desire for them to be real by refusing to wear the plastic mask of Christian perfection. To accomplish this in our kids, we need to be men and women who are passionate about the gospel and who are growing in faith as disciples. We need to be humble and ready to admit we desperately need the gospel. Lastly, we must be committed to the gospel, willing to do whatever it takes to bring glory to God.

CHAPTER 29

GOSPEL MISSION: THE KIDS LEADER AS A MISSIONARY

How long did it take you to figure out that serving in kids ministry is so much more than teaching once a week? Probably not long. Teaching for an hour or so is just the tip of the iceberg. Each week you likely spend additional hours studying the session's content, adapting it to fit your kids and your context, praying over your kids and what they will hear, and collecting the supplies you'll need for the week.

Then there's the time spent outside the classroom that involves going to soccer games and dance recitals with your kids and their families and writing birthday cards and notes when your kids miss a week. Add to that all of the other kids ministry events and activities that you attend and help with.

Yes, your schedule is full. "No Rest for the Weary" could be the slogan for those of us already serving.

If we aren't careful, kids ministry can wear us out. There are just so many needs, and it's hard for us to say no to our kids. We want to be there for them—as much as we can—because serving in kids ministry is one of the ways we live on mission. It's one of the main ways we respond to the gospel transformation taking place in us. This is why it's hard to not keep going one hundred miles an hour in ministry.

Here's the truth though: if we're running on empty, we have nothing to give our kids. We need to guard time in which we can rest, spend time with Christ, and grow. Does that sound selfish to you? It shouldn't. It's exactly what Jesus (the model of selflessness) did.

> **But the news about him spread even more, and large crowds would come together to hear him and to be healed of their sicknesses. Yet he often withdrew to deserted places and prayed. (Luke 5:15–16)**

Notice how Luke couples these two verses with the word *yet*. Large crowds came to Jesus and needed Him; what a ministry opportunity! Yet, He would often walk away from public ministry to get by Himself and pray. Jesus needed to get away, recharge, and spend time with His Father. If Jesus needed to do this, why do we think we don't?

When we try to serve in kids ministry on empty, we will not point our kids to the gospel. We will only be able to point them to ourselves. As we have seen, the gospel transforms. It transforms our kids and it transforms us. This transformation doesn't happen automatically or in a vacuum. Gospel transformation takes place when we spend time with Christ and let Him drive the gospel more deeply into our minds and hearts. Then, and only then, will the Holy Spirit produce the fruit of gospel change.

Do you see the problem? If we aren't spending time in the gospel as kids leaders, we are short-circuiting gospel transformation in our lives. The painful irony of this is that our attempt to teach the gospel to our kids in our own power will actually block the gospel. When we try to serve in our own power, we serve contrary to the core message of the gospel. That message is that we desperately need Jesus and His power to change us and advance His ministry.

This is why it is critical that we guard regular time for our own growth as kids leaders. It's not selfish; it's actually selfless as we empty ourselves before God. Doing this is not optional! We can't make any excuses. Ministry is always going to be busy. Our kids are always going to need something. However, they don't need us; they need the gospel working through us. This will only happen if we're growing as disciples ourselves.

Protect your daily time alone with God. Make sure you're part of an adult small group—don't let your kids be your small group! Meet regularly with two or three other adults, preferably from outside of kids ministry (so you don't end up talking "work" all the time) for encouragement and accountability.

Now, I know what you might be thinking. "Where am I going to get the time to do all this? I can barely keep my head above the water as it is! It isn't reasonable to add these obligations to my already overcrowded plate."

I hear you. Really, I do! But we need to get to the point where we realize that serving on empty is what is truly unreasonable. We need to do whatever it takes to protect the gospel transformation in our own lives, even if that means choosing not do some kids ministry programs.

Remember that Jesus' earthly ministry lasted a scant three years. He certainly had a good reason to squeeze every minute of His schedule to meet the needs of the people who came to Him. But He didn't. At times, He strategically walked away from ministry, as busy as He was, because He knew He couldn't fulfill His mission apart from the Father. He knew He couldn't do it on His own. And neither can we.

Questions for Reflection and Discussion

- Do you see yourself as a theologian? Why or why not?
- How has the gospel changed you this past month? Year?
- When was the last time you used a personal story of your growth as you taught kids?
- How do you protect personal time to be with Christ each day? What do you do during these times?

Application: Gospel-Centered Leaders

1. **Develop and implement a leader recruiting strategy for the ministry.** Consider your leadership recruitment and development process for four basic stages:

- *Recruiting:* What is the non-negotiable essentials for serving in your kids ministry? What are the preferences beyond those? How do you recruit leaders? What is the "ask"?
- *Onboarding:* What type of leadership application do you use? How do you interview potential leaders? Conduct background checks? How do you train new leaders once they have been approved?
- *Serving:* How do you train new leaders so that they are positioned for success? How do you train existing leaders at least annually? What policies and procedures are in place? Do any need to be changed or added?
- *Offboarding:* What type of exit interview do you conduct? How do you thank them for their service? Is there a path for them to reengage in serving if they choose?

2. **Develop and conduct an annual time of vision-casting and encouragement for your leaders.** Your leaders cannot hear the vision of the ministry enough, and no one can be encouraged and thanked enough. Plan and hold a time to do this—at least once per year. Do not add anything else to the agenda—guard this time for these two critical objectives. Consider making these times as special as possible for your leaders, perhaps including a nice meal and some form of a gift of appreciation.

3. **Develop and implement a spiritual growth plan for your leaders.** Consider books and resources on theology, ministry, spiritual growth, etc., for you and your team to

read. Develop a realistic, yet ambitious, calendar for reading these resources together and some way to interact and share what was learned. This might be gathering the entire team together, having small groups of leaders meet on their own, or connecting digitally.

PART 6

GOSPEL-CENTERED PARENTS

CHAPTER 30

PARENTING 101: THE SHEMA

The children of the first generation of Israelites who had come out of Egypt were at the border of the Promised Land at last. Because of their parents' disobedience, Israel had wandered in the wilderness for forty years and the entire older generation had died off (except for Joshua, Caleb, and Moses). Now Moses, who was forbidden from entering the land because of his sin, was saying his farewell to the people and transferring leadership to Joshua.

During this transition, Moses restated the law one more time for the people to hear. He knew that their absolute obedience to God was essential to their success in the land. At the heart of Moses' retelling of the law is a passage about parenting known as the *Shema*—the Hebrew word for listen:

**"Listen, Israel: The Lord our God, the Lord is one."
(Deut. 6:4)**

The passage begins with a theological statement about God's oneness. God was reminding His people that He is unique—there is none like Him. With this statement, God invited Israel to remember who He is and what He had done. They were to remember how God had provided for and protected His people and how He alone is the all powerful Creator. They remembered that God was good, gracious, merciful, and kind.

Remembering who God is and what He had done would naturally lead to the next part of the Shema:

"Love the Lord your God with all your heart, with all your soul, and with all your strength." (Deut. 6:5)

The more we reflect on who God is and what He has done, that is, the more we get to know God, the more we will love Him. A heart being transformed by the gospel will grow in love for God as it grows in the knowledge and remembrance of God.

Notice that God told His people to internalize His words:

"These words that I am giving you today are to be in your heart." (Deut. 6:6)

The more we know God and love Him, the more we understand and trust His heart behind His commands. We come to know and trust that all of God's commands are for

His glory and our good, even if they may not feel that way at times.

We are already three verses into the Shema, but notice God has yet to give any instruction about parenting—everything to this point is about a parent's relationship with God. Parents can't pass along something they don't already have. If a parent is going to lead their child into a vibrant relationship with God, the parent has to have a meaningful relationship with God himself.

With that point established, it's now time to give parents a practical blueprint for how to disciple their children:

> **"Repeat them [God's words] to your children. Talk about them when you sit in your house and when you walk along the road, when you lie down and when you get up." (Deut. 6:7)**

In other words, parents are to talk about God's Word all the time to their kids. God intends parents to talk about Him as a natural part of their rhythm of life. Speaking about the gospel should be a regular part of our daily routine.

God should be such a regular part of a family's daily life that the family is marked by their love for Him:

> Parents are to talk about God's Word all the time to their kids. God intends parents to talk about Him as a natural part of their rhythm of life.

"Bind them as a sign on your hand and let them be a symbol on your forehead. Write them on the doorposts of your house and on your city gates" (Deut. 6:8–9).

Some Jews took these instructions literally and wrote Scripture on small pieces of paper, placing the tiny scrolls in small boxes called phylacteries. The phylacteries were then banded to their wrists and foreheads. However, God was more concerned with His Word guiding what His people thought (symbolized by their foreheads) and did (symbolized by their hands) than with physical adornment. God's Word would also define their homes, much like how a street address marks our homes today.

> God was more concerned with His Word guiding what His people thought (symbolized by their foreheads) and did (symbolized by their hands) than with physical adornment.

The Shema can be summarized in three sentences: 1) Know who God is—gospel teaching. 2) Love God with all your heart—gospel transformation. 3) Let your love for God change your life and mark how you live—gospel mission.

Once again we see the familiar pattern—the same pattern we need to base our kids ministries on and the pattern we need to base our leadership on. This is God's calling to parents as the primary shepherds over their children's lives. This is what our kids ministries need to encourage and equip parents to do.

CHAPTER 31

HOME AND CHURCH

Have you ever noticed how the church in America loves to overreact? When we realize there's a problem in the church, we have this tendency to respond with hyper-aggression and move as far in the opposite direction as we can. Kind of like Jonah.

The church is too wooden and formulaic? We'll get rid of all structure! Church buildings are too large and elaborate? We'll meet in a warehouse or maybe even a tent! We meet needs without sharing the gospel? We'll just share the gospel and not meet needs!

What we often do is simply exchange one problem for another. If only we could learn to find the balance in the middle. The relationship between the church and the home is another one of these areas where we have seen the pendulum swing wildly to extremes.

When I was growing up in the 1970s and '80s, the church acted as the primary disciple-making influence for kids. That may not have been stated explicitly, but it was how most churches and families acted. Parents would take their kids to the trained professionals at the church to teach them about God in the same way that they took them to the trained professionals at school or to music instructors.

Then, at some point, a movement began to sweep through the church to restore the home as the primary place for teaching kids the gospel. But once again, many churches took the movement too far and basically handed off this role to parents with little or no guidance and equipping.

> **We have many parents today who recognize it's primarily their responsibility to shepherd their kids.**

The result is that we have many parents today who recognize it's primarily their responsibility to shepherd their kids. However, these parents often don't know where to begin. We have parents in our churches who are frustrated and feel like they're failing miserably. At the same time, we have many kids leaders and pastors who assume that parents are failing in their roles. The only perceived option is to leave the job to "the professionals."

As is often the case, the solution lies between the two extremes. We have to meet in the middle. Kids ministry leaders and parents have to find a way to work together to provide a comprehensive discipleship plan for our kids.

There is too much at risk. Our kids are too important. We need to learn from that same second generation that came out of Egypt:

> Joshua son of Nun, the servant of the Lord, died at the age of 110. They buried him in the territory of his inheritance, in Timnath-heres, in the hill country of Ephraim, north of Mount Gaash. That whole generation was also gathered to their ancestors. After them another generation rose up who did not know the Lord or the works he had done for Israel. The Israelites did what was evil in the Lord's sight. They worshiped the Baals and abandoned the Lord, the God of their fathers, who had brought them out of Egypt. They followed other gods from the surrounding peoples and bowed down to them. They angered the Lord, for they abandoned him and worshiped Baal and the Ashtoreths. The Lord's anger burned against Israel, and he handed them over to marauders who raided them. He sold them to the enemies around them, and they could no longer resist their enemies. Whenever the Israelites went out, the Lord was against them and brought disaster on them, just as he had promised and sworn to them. So they suffered greatly. (Judg. 2:8–15)

It should haunt us, parents and kids leaders alike, that a people two generations removed from the exodus would abandon God. We don't know exactly how this happened, but it did. The second generation failed to teach the next generation about God and what He had done for them. They failed to live out the Shema. As a result, their children did evil and turned away from God and toward idolatry.

But God is a jealous God, and He disciplined His people out of His love for them.[32] The great suffering He brought on His people was for their good. God wanted His people to turn back to Him in their distress.

Our kids will be on a similar path if kids leaders and parents fail to work together, encourage one another, and equip and support one another. As we saw earlier, the statistics show that about 70 percent of our kids will turn away from God after they leave student ministry. God may even bring suffering into their lives to turn them back to Him, just like He did with Israel.

Of course, there is also the risk that kids won't respond to God's discipline and will turn from Him for good. This possibility should motivate us to do whatever it takes to make sure that parents are embracing their vital responsibility to make disciples of their kids.

32. Proverbs 3:12; Hebrews 12:6.

CHAPTER 32

GOSPEL TEACHING: PARTNERING WITH PARENTS AS THEOLOGIANS

God's plan for parents is that they be the primary shepherds over their kids. Unfortunately, instead of receiving the life-giving, life-changing gospel, many kids receive oppressive legalism or cultural Christianity. Paul writes:

> Children, obey your parents in the Lord, because this is right. Honor your father and mother, which is the first commandment with a promise, so that it may go well with you and that you may have a long life in the land. Fathers, don't stir up anger

in your children, but bring them up in the training and instruction of the Lord. (Eph. 6:1–4)

Sometimes what doesn't appear in Scripture is just as important as what does. For example, notice that in this passage, the word *only* isn't used. God didn't command parents to be the *only* disciple-makers of kids, but the primary disciple-makers as the ones who love their kids the most and spend the most time with them.

Ideally, our kids ministries should echo what has already been taught in the home. We should celebrate when we hear our kids say they already know a Bible story, or Jesus, or the gospel, because their parents told it to them.

However, it's not fair of us to expect parents to know what to do in the home automatically. Knowing how to teach kids the gospel doesn't come automatically to a person as soon as he or she becomes a parent. This is why we need to partner with parents to help them develop as theologians. We need to coach parents on the what, when, how, and even the why of sharing the gospel with kids.

Equipping parents to disciple their kids begins long before they have kids—actually before they even get married. The foundation of godly parenting is a godly marriage. The foundation of a godly marriage is understanding our call to glorify God in everything we do.[33] God wants young adults to grow in the gospel, in part, so that if He calls them to parenthood later on, they can be equipped to shepherd the children God puts in their care.

---

33. 1 Corinthians 10:31.

Take a step back with me for a moment and look at God's comprehensive discipleship design. Preschoolers and kids learn the gospel—God's big story of the Bible—and experience heart transformation and changed lives. They grow to become students and young adults who continue to look at the gospel more deeply and appreciate it more fully.

These young adults may eventually marry and have kids of their own whom they disciple. This starts the process all over again.

So what can we as kids leaders do for parents to help them in this critical role? Praying for them is a great start. Pray that your parents embrace their role as disciple-makers of their children. Pray that they grow and experience a vibrant relationship with Christ. Pray that they are intentional in their discipleship and that they take advantage of the daily opportunities to talk with their kids about Jesus.

> **Pray that they are intentional in their discipleship and that they take advantage of the daily opportunities to talk with their kids about Jesus.**

In addition to praying regularly for your parents, strive to be a Barnabas (that is, an encouraging influence) for them. Make it your goal to encourage them regularly. Parenting is rough! It's draining and is plagued with feelings of doubt and inadequacy. Speak words of life to your parents. Remind them of their calling to parent their kids with the gospel. Encourage them to avoid the traps of the world and to instill gospel-centered worth in their kids based on who they are in Christ rather than what they can do. Encourage them to parent with grace—giving it freely to their kids and clinging desperately to it in their own lives. Be the kind of leader parents want to be around!

Another practical way to partner with parents is to inform them of what is being taught at church. Parents should know what Bible stories and big ideas you are covering, now and in the weeks ahead. This knowledge allows parents to proactively engage their kids in conversations related to what will be covered. It also allows parents to review what was taught to their kids.

> **Grow together as you work together to raise up kids who know the gospel and love Christ.**

Remember, kids leaders and parents should both be growing as theologians, so why not do it together? Share books and resources, and perhaps even develop reading discussion groups made up of leaders and parents. Grow together as you work together to raise up kids who know the gospel and love Christ.

CHAPTER 33

GOSPEL TRANSFORMATION: PARTNERING WITH PARENTS AS DISCIPLES

This may sound counterintuitive to pretty much everything we have covered to this point, but here goes. Parents have to know the Old Testament law and teach it to their kids.

Why would I say that? Doesn't that go against teaching the gospel? Isn't this at odds with concepts like grace and one's identity in Christ? Not at all. It's just a matter of why it's important to know the law. We need to know the law so that we can understand the pervasive nature of sin in our own hearts. Consider how Paul puts it:

> **What should we say then? Is the law sin?**
> **Absolutely not! On the contrary, I would not have**
> **known sin if it were not for the law. For example,**
> **I would not have known what it is to covet if the**
> **law had not said, Do not covet. (Rom. 7:7)**

So an understanding of the law helps us come to terms with our sin, and coming to terms with sin enables us to understand and appreciate grace. Parents who want to disciple their kids should strive to maintain a posture of humility and awe toward God's work in their own lives. A kid will learn more from a parent's yielded and contrite gospel-centered heart than anything else that parent will say. There's power in modeling a life continually changed by the gospel.

This is what Jesus had in mind when the Pharisees scorned Him for allowing a woman to wash and anoint His feet.

> **Then one of the Pharisees invited him to eat**
> **with him. He entered the Pharisee's house and**
> **reclined at the table. And a woman in the town who**
> **was a sinner found out that Jesus was reclining at**
> **the table in the Pharisee's house. She brought an**
> **alabaster jar of perfume and stood behind him at**
> **his feet, weeping, and began to wash his feet with**
> **her tears. She wiped his feet with her hair, kissing**
> **them and anointing them with the perfume.**
>
> **When the Pharisee who had invited him saw**
> **this, he said to himself, "This man, if he were a**
> **prophet, would know who and what kind of woman**
> **this is who is touching him—she's a sinner!"**

Jesus replied to him, "Simon, I have something to say to you."

He said, "Say it, teacher."

"A creditor had two debtors. One owed five hundred denarii, and the other fifty. Since they could not pay it back, he graciously forgave them both. So, which of them will love him more?"

Simon answered, "I suppose the one he forgave more."

"You have judged correctly," he told him. Turning to the woman, he said to Simon, "Do you see this woman? I entered your house; you gave me no water for my feet, but she, with her tears, has washed my feet and wiped them with her hair. You gave me no kiss, but she hasn't stopped kissing my feet since I came in. You didn't anoint my head with olive oil, but she has anointed my feet with perfume. Therefore I tell you, her many sins have been forgiven; that's why she loved much. But the one who is forgiven little, loves little." Then he said to her, "Your sins are forgiven." (Luke 7:36–48)

The Pharisees looked at who the woman had been. Jesus looked at who she had become. The Pharisees viewed the great sin they saw as a barrier. Jesus looked at the great sin that was forgiven. So did the woman. Great love flows from a heart that recognizes it has been forgiven greatly.

Knowing this truth and living it out is what will fuel a parent's discipleship and, by extension, their gospel-centered parenting. This is what we need to encourage parents to remember. Just as we want to teach from the overflow of what God is doing in our lives, the best parenting also comes from gospel overflow.

So how can we encourage gospel-centered parenting like this? A great way is to foster an environment that celebrates parenting and gives parents opportunities to grow and develop in community. Build into your normal ministry times for celebrating the role of parents. Many churches have a parent-child dedication for infants and their parents. We should also look for ways to honor and encourage other parenting milestones. Look for ways to honor grandparents too. They are often forgotten in churches but play an important role. Strive to communicate that God prioritizes parenting in your church.

Along with celebrating and valuing parenting, be sure to provide different opportunities for parents to continue to grow. Parenting-based small groups, parenting mentorships, and parenting conferences and retreats should be offered regularly. Foster an environment where parents can readily admit that they're far from perfect and where participating in parenting groups isn't a sign of failure. Involvement in these groups is an indication that parents are being shaped and formed by God and that they desire to point their kids to the gospel.

CHAPTER 34

GOSPEL MISSION: PARTNERING WITH PARENTS AS MISSIONARIES

I have to admit that when I hear *missionary*, it is hard for me not to think immediately of someone serving God in Africa or Asia. That is my knee-jerk reaction to that word even though I know that every follower of Jesus is called to be a missionary, even if it's just down the street.

I have to force myself to think more broadly of *missionary*—more biblically—to include my country, my state, and even my neighborhood. But do you see how I still stopped short? I failed to include my home. Even when I remember that God has me on mission at my job, at the local grocery store, and even in my neighborhood, I still often fail to remember that God has me on mission in my home. And that mission—as a husband and father—is my most important one.

This is why one of the greatest things we can do as kids leaders is remind our parents of their primary mission in the home and do whatever we can to encourage them and support them. A good place to start is to take a passage we often use to support the value of kids ministry and apply it to the home.

> **Then children were brought to Jesus for him to place his hands on them and pray, but the disciples rebuked them. Jesus said, "Leave the children alone, and don't try to keep them from coming to me, because the kingdom of heaven belongs to such as these." (Matt. 19:13–14)**

This passage is often used to cast vision for kids ministry in the local church. We don't want our churches to create any barriers that prevent kids from coming to Jesus. This is certainly true and is a fair way to teach this passage. However, how often do we think about what Jesus said in the context of the home? Are there any barriers that parents can place between their kids and Jesus?

One such barrier occurs when parents abdicate their ministry to make a disciple of their child. It's not enough for parents to bring a kid to church. It isn't even enough for parents to affirm what is taught at church. God intends for parents to take the lead in disciple-making. To do this, they need to see themselves as missionaries in their own home.

We need to help each parent in our ministry know this truth and embrace it. This is one of the reasons I'm such a big advocate of Bible study curriculum that is aligned in some manner for all ages—preschool, kids, students, and adults. When we align all of our age groups around Bible story, biblical truth, or Bible book, we help position our parents to engage in meaningful discipleship in the home. What parents learn in their Bible study groups benefits them and also helps prepare them to talk with their kids. Aligning all our age groups makes it easier for parents to be the disciple-makers they need to be in the home. When this happens, it's a big win for parents, for the church, and for our communities.

There are three other ways our kids ministries can help parents be on mission in the home. First, we can engage in ongoing conversations about some of the difficult stories in the Bible and the challenging aspects of the gospel. What a kid hears at church should echo what she has already heard in the home. Anticipate the sessions that may be a little more challenging and let your parents know in advance what is being covered, why it is being covered, and how it is being covered. This will give your

> **What a kid hears at church should echo what she has already heard in the home.**

parents increased confidence in the ministry and also equip them to lead similar conversations in the home.

Second, we can be careful to provide balanced kids ministries that offer opportunities for kids and families while still giving plenty of space for families to be families. We have to be careful not to program our ministries so much that parents are left without the time they need to disciple their kids and be on mission in their neighborhoods.

Third, we can remind parents that they're raising missionaries. Look how God describes kids:

> **Sons are indeed a heritage from the LORD, offspring, a reward. Like arrows in the hand of a warrior are the sons born in one's youth. Happy is the man who has filled his quiver with them. They will never be put to shame when they speak with their enemies at the city gate. (Ps. 127:3–5)**

Children are a reward—a blessing from God. But they aren't just for a parent's joy—they are also given for a purpose—to be arrows. Kids aren't trinkets to be placed on a shelf to be looked at every once in awhile and dusted. They are gospel messengers entrusted to parents by God. We need to encourage parents to be on mission as they steward this precious gift well.

Questions for Reflection and Discussion

- What do you see as the parents' role in leading kids to be disciples? What do you see as the church's role?
- Parents who disciple their children well are not guaranteed that their kids will become disciples.

How can you encourage parents whose children do not follow Jesus?

- How do you teach parents of preschoolers to disciple their kids from birth?
- What discipleship plan does your kids ministry have for kids who come from homes without believing parents?
- What do you do to include, value, and celebrate all kinds of families? Grandparents? Foster families? Families who have adopted or are pursuing adoption? Single parents?
- How do you disciple and equip parents? Do parents know what their children are learning at church each week and why? How can you do this better?

Application: Gospel-Centered Parents

1. **Curate and share gospel-centered resources for families.** Consider what books and resources would be helpful for families to support them in their role of discipleship in the home. Keep an updated list of these resources available for families, and perhaps develop a library of the resources themselves.

2. **Develop and implement a strategic plan for moving kids through your preschool, kids, and student ministries.** Work with all of the ministry leaders involved with kids through students (family pastor, kids pastor, student pastor, etc) and develop a comprehensive discipleship strategy to guide this process from start to finish. What should

kids learn and experience? Share this plan with parents and think of ways to encourage and support their discipleship in the home.

3. **Conduct family celebrations during the year.** Seek to be family champions and look for ways to recognize and celebrate key transitions and events for families such as the birth of children and birthdays, adoptions and gotcha days, marriages, starting school, transition to middle school, etc.

4. **Evaluate your ministry calendar.** Put your ministry calendar under the microscope. Are you too busy and separating families from each other too much? Are you not doing enough for families? Can you identify a clear gospel-related win for every single activity and event on your calendar? Add what needs to be added, change what needs to be changed, and delete what needs to be deleted.

CONCLUSION

When was the last time you took a roll of film to be developed? It's probably been quite a while, hasn't it? I can't even remember the last time I saw a place that develops film! Digital photography has basically rendered printed film obsolete and nearly destroyed Kodak, the once mighty behemoth of the film industry.

It makes sense that digital photography would hurt a company like Kodak the most, but did you know that Kodak invented the digital camera? Or that Kodak knew the potential impact digital photography could make on the printed film industry all the way back in the early 1980s? Kodak was in the perfect position to lead a global shift into the age of digital photography.

But instead of doing that, the company made a disastrous decision—to use the new digital photography technology to improve its film-based products, like the 1996 Advantix Preview system. The Advantix used a digital viewer so users could preview the pictures they took and decide which pictures . . . to print to film. I'm sure that decision made complete sense to Kodak's executives since everything they did centered on printing pictures on photo paper.[34]

Needless to say, the Advantix failed and Kodak's stock took a prolonged nosedive because of the very technology the company had invented and so grossly misunderstood.

Kodak saw the danger. Kodak was in the perfect position to adapt. But they didn't. And they missed the opportunity to dominate the digital photography industry.

The church and her kids ministries are currently in a position like the one Kodak was in thirty years ago. We see the danger of moralistic Bible teaching. We see the danger of behavior modification. We see the danger of viewing kids as the church of tomorrow. We see the danger of lowered expectations for kids leaders. We see the danger of a rift between the church and the home.

And at the same time, we see the potential of the gospel to transform our kids. We recognize the opportunity of being at the forefront of seeing God work majestically in and through our kids as they experience the fullness of the gospel. We see the beauty and power of a gospel-centered kids ministry.

So what will we do? What will you do? Will we cling to methods, structures, and visions that have proven to be lacking? Or will we do whatever it takes to proclaim the gospel and give our kids Jesus? Will we do whatever it takes to be gospel-centered?

---

34. Chunka Mui, "How Kodak Failed," *Forbes*, 18 January 2012 [6 February 2017]. Available on the Internet: http://www.forbes.com.

There's so much more at stake than stock prices and photography equipment. What we do will impact our kids, our families, our churches, our communities, and our world.

This is why failure is not an option.

ABOUT THE AUTHOR

Brian Dembowczyk served in church ministry for sixteen years, including time as a children's, student, and family pastor, and now serves as managing editor for The Gospel Project at LifeWay Christian Resources. Brian earned a D.Min. from the New Orleans Baptist Theological Seminary, an M.Div. from the Southern Baptist Theological Seminary, and is pursuing a Ph.D. from the Midwestern Baptist Theolgoical Seminary. Brian and his wife, Tara, live in Murfreesboro, Tennessee, with their three children: Joshua, Hannah, and Caleb.